EPIC

101 Short Stories, Essays, and Insights to Improve Communication Skills

TABLE OF CONTENTS

AUTHORS PREFACE

I run a YouTube channel called ArmaniTalks.
Every now and then, I watch old videos of myself.

'That's so egotistical bro!'
Actually, the exact opposite.

Athletes have always fascinated me.
Whenever I'm bored, I watch an interview of a top-tier athlete.
One thing they often say is:
'I watch a lot of film.'

Average athletes don't say that.
But the great ones do.

Why do they watch film?
- It's to reduce the ego's grasp over them.

The ego tends to play up the strengths and downplay the weaknesses.
But the tape doesn't lie.
It shows if you dropped the ball or did a good job.

> **The tape takes the subjective element out of it and introduces objectivity.**

So, I cringe watching these old videos.
My body fights me on it.

Neurologically, we are not wired to watch ourselves on tape.

It's because we normally see life from a 1st-person point of view.

When we see ourselves in 3rd perspective, the nervous system is like:

'*MAKE IT STOPP!!!!*'

Over time, the nervous system gets used to it.

Watching film becomes therapeutic.

One evening, I stumbled across a video where I talked about the magic of thinking big.

In this video, I tell a story about a father and son.

Long story short, the father is disappointed in the son.

He believes his son isn't living to his full potential.

Always playing video games and sleeping.

One day, the father walks into his son's room and says:

'*Son, you will be joining me at work this weekend. You will be giving a speech to my company. There will be 5,000 people in attendance.*'

The son is terrified.

5,000 people?

That's so many!

Immediately, the son's heartbeat rises, his palms get sweaty, and his mouth gets dry.

The son begs his father not to make him give the speech.

But the father is adamant.

For the next few days, the son practices the talk over and over.

Each time he pictures the gargantuan audience, each time he gets nervous.

As the days pass, the fear reduces, and acceptance takes its place.
Although he is still nervous, he has now come to terms with his fate.

On speech day, the father walks the son to the entrance of the stadium.
The dad is going to introduce him.
Before the dad walks in to introduce his son, he asks:
'Ready?'

The son nods.

The dad walks in, gives an introduction, and calls his son in.
There is a roar of applause.
The son walks into the stadium.

And there it is!!
50 people.

Once the son sees that he is going to give a speech in front of 50 people, he looks at his dad.
His dad is laughing.

The son gives the speech with fire.
He has so much extra energy because he thought he was going to be giving the talk to a MUCH larger audience.

That story was meant to highlight the value of **gargantuan thinking.**
How thoughts have practical effects on your daily actions.

The person who has the vision of becoming a billionaire in the future will work significantly different than someone who is working towards $100,000.

This is why I love the field of creativity.

Not just like it.

But it's a field that I've grown to love.

In 2012, I had 2 choices for an internship.

- Be an electrical engineer in a biomedical technology company.
- Or a systems engineer in an aerospace company.

Since I was in the college of electrical engineering, I was expected to go with the 1st path.

My college advisor **strongly** suggested that I choose the 1st path.

Not to sound corny.

- But my heart told me to choose the latter path.

My classmates and advisor told me that a systems engineer wasn't really an engineer.

It was a knockoff.

I understood why they said that.

It's because a systems engineer is a hybrid of the technical **and** business field.

The problem with a lot of engineering projects is that the teams' work solo.

This leads to a lot of miscommunication and bugs when the solo teams are expected to deliver 1 fully functioning deliverable.

Therefore, the systems engineer was introduced.

They were supposed to speak the language of the engineers to cross-communicate messages among the teams.

But a project doesn't only exist in the technical realm.
You have budgets to work with.
Stakeholders to satisfy.
And occasional office politics to play.

> **The systems engineer needs to speak machine language and human language.**

The fascinating thing about the role is that it *trains* a person to see the BIGGER picture.

A lot of engineers would get obsessed with the code.
They thought the code was everything.

They didn't remotely understand the importance of the hardware.
Quality assurance.
Project managers.
Sales.
Clients.
None of that.

For them, it was just their precious code.
- Ego-centered thinking.

The systems engineer understood the bigger picture.
- Us-centered thinking.

That's creativity in a nutshell:
-Understand the bigger picture.

Steve Jobs felt guilty for being dubbed a creative genius.
He thought his insights were common sense.

That's because his worldview was larger than his peers.

The stories in this book are meant to fuel your creative spirit.

What better way to do that than improve your communication skills?

Humans are nodes.

Communication skills allow you to effectively connect the nodes.

But why communicate average thoughts?

Let's go **gargantuan**.

Quit doing so much market research.

Quit being like all these other people.

Be unique.

In *EPIC*, you will be given 101 short stories to develop introspection skills, build a thick skin, and harness/articulate creative thoughts.

This will allow you to be in a lane of your own.

Many will try to copy you.

But a few will succeed.

Scratch that, **no one** will succeed.

Because you're operating within a completely different ruleset.

It's out of this world.

– ARMANITALKS

MEMORY

Memory is a gift & a curse.
It's a technology as well.

To make memory a servant is wise.
To make memory a master is foolish.

When analyzing the mind, it's easy to get carried away.
Especially when not living in the present.

In modern times, getting to a present state is earned.
Although we are naturally present people.
That's the baseline state.

It's like the dirty room example.

The room is naturally clean.
But since a bunch of our friends came this past weekend for the tailgate...it's now messy.

Beer bottles, chips & wrappers everywhere.
Dirty.

-The correct step would be to clean the room.
-The incorrect step would be to say that the room has always been dirty.

The baseline state was clean and now it's our journey to get back to that.

This may not seem fair.

I mean this guy's friends dirtied his room.
Why should he clean it??

Because it's his room.

Likewise, if we are naturally present people...then why do I need
to TRAIN myself to get back to my natural state?

Because, busy society dirtied it.

Living in the information age is a game of our mind being pulled
in all directions.
And a journey of building a mental plan to keep bringing it back
to a location.

When the elbow grease is put in, now memory can serve as a
servant.
We can draw into the reserves at will.

'And if we don't put the work in?'
Then we identify with memory.

That's the pretty scary thing.
When past mistakes happen in different contexts...
Any idea why?

It's because new life experiences are being filtered thru the past.
Also known as **sleepwalking thru life.**

Identifying with the memory is one of the dumbest things to do...
Because the memory can be a drama queen at times.

A moment from your past which was not that BAD...

May get amplified into the boogie monster because the memory
just wants to create a show.

You got a memory like that?

Something you logically know wasn't that bad..
But still, your body acts like it was worse.

This is why the memory does not make a good master.
It's a game of training it to be beneath us.
'How?'
Thru practice.

There are infinite ways to practice taming your memory.
Few include:
 *puzzles, writing, remembering interesting little details,
recalling memories from the past etc.*

Which ever path is chosen does not matter too much.
What matters the most is the act of **commanding the mind.**

That's why "discipline" is an amazing word.
The word in itself sounds eh.
But it's a phrase for "program yourself."

The act of YOU willingly recalling something from your memory
bank tells the memory that it's a servant, not the master.

And momentarily, there is a *gap*.

The memory is a faculty of the mind.
Yet, there is something that is commanding the mind.

How can the mind command the mind?

No, this is **awareness** commanding the mind.
Awareness is the mind's boss.

Allowing the mind to command the mind is like letting a rascal manage himself.
Pass.

Get a higher authority that follows a different ruleset to manage that rascal.
That's the awareness in this case.

Each time the memory is commanded, each time it is tamed.

When the memory becomes tamed, it becomes a goldmine..
Especially in the era of information and content creation.

With a weak memory, it's hard to be creative.
With a strong memory, it's hard not to be creative.

KNOWING WHEN TO STOP

It's tax season.
And it's time to file taxes.

Filing taxes is a necessary evil.
For business owners (let alone anyone) it can be a pain in the ass.
Get the documents, organize it & arrange a few meetings.

My tax guy is the same one from last year.
Tom.

Tom and I get along.
He's a guy in his 60's who has been an accountant for over 20 years.

Last year, he discovered my YouTube channel & says that he watches it.
Whenever I go to his office, he says:
'When ArmaniTalks, people listen.'

This is our way of setting off the meeting.

After our 2nd meeting this year to finalize some stuff, I noticed his coworker.

Tom's coworker looks just like him.
And both have a similar, jolly attitude.

Last time I went to the office, Tom's coworker was assisting a couple.

The couple was in their 50s.

This couple was loud and very talkative.
The wife being the louder and the more talkative one.

It was evident that they had a very wild year last year.
Especially in terms of real estate.

They did a whole bunch of real estate deals, and now had to get the tax person up to speed.

This couple sat in the cube next to Tom and me...

They were so loud that it was often hard to hear to Tom.
I had to lean my ear to the glass multiple times and be like:
 'say that again.'

There came a point when the wife was telling a story about their recent transaction.

And I kid you not...
She was going thru EVERY detail.

"And I called the guy.
He said no the first day.
The next day he said no to meeting up.
The third day he agreed to show us the listing.
I found the listing in this website.
On and on and on...."

It seemed like Tom's coworker was too nice to be like, shut the fuck up already!
You're actually making my job harder with all your incessant rambling.

But no.
He was a chill guy, remember?

Eventually, the husband butts in and is like:
'So to wrap it up, we bought the property.'

The husband summarized the wife's incessant rambling in a
powerful fashion.

Tom's coworker seemed like he was just given a life jacket.
He seemed like he gave the husband the thank you eyes.
When you subtly nod your head at someone.

Everyone seemed pleased.
Besides the wife.

The wife angrily asks the husband:
'Why would you ruin my story like that?'

And for the rest of the meeting, she showed visibly irritated body
language.
Scowled eye brows, arms crossed & reduced torso.

Story???

Lady, I don't know what the hell you were saying.
But that definitely was not a story!

In this situation, who was wrong?
The wife for rambling too much...
Or the husband for cutting her off?

Before immediately blaming the wife...

We need to understand a crucial point.

Storytelling is a skillset.

It's not something that you just learn willy nilly.
It requires a bit of practice & a whole bunch of self awareness.

Only then can a story get polished and give the consumer some meaning.

Unfortunately for the wife, she fell in the boat of someone who does not have a clue on how to tell a story.

In her mind, nothing was wrong.
This was her version of telling her tale.

Although Tom's coworker and her husband were able to immediately spot the rambling and the excessive details...
She was blind to it.

It's like she was sitting in a room in pitch black darkness.
That's what blind means in terms of information.

To add to the dilemma of spotting who was wrong in this situation...
We don't really know the husband & wife's relationship behind the scenes.

No clue to assess rapport, normal talking patterns and comfort levels, based on the small interaction in the tax office.

So it's best to say that neither party was wrong.

Hopefully, she was able to build self awareness from the situation afterwards.

Once the anger subsided.

When someone gets excessively detailed, no one wins.
Even the person talking will talk themselves into a headache.

Knowing when to stop is much harder than it looks.

Self improvement normally talks about how to begin something.

-Go on buddy...just start.
-A goal without a deadline is just a wish.
-1 percent progress is still progress..

Those kind of quotes.

On the flipside, storytelling is all about knowing **when to stop** .
Beginning plays a role.
But the money is at stopping something.

Just like I am about to stop now.
Bye bye.

CHANGING VIEW OF TIME

I once saw this Matthew McConaughey talk where he was speaking about delayed gratification.

I don't remember the exact details.
But remember enough to see how he viewed time.

When he won an Oscar, it was a big deal.
Not for the award..
But for the lesson he was able to teach his children.

His kids asked him:
'Daddy, did you JUST win an award for that film you were filming a couple of months back?'

And with conviction, he said yes.
He wanted to emphasize how he was reaping the fruits LATER.

He put in work in the past, and was not immediately rewarded.
However, his time came.

Matthew was trying to drill home the concept of delayed gratification.
Plant the seeds now & allow the crops to grow.

I have a less glamorous example of this.

Whenever I write a blog, I have a few keywords in the blog which I can link to a past blog.

Example:
Let's say I write a blog called, *"What is Toastmasters?"*

And somewhere in the blog, I write:

Toastmasters is a club which exercises public speaking. A few ways to exercise public speaking is through planned speeches, Table Topics & evaluations.

From looking at that paragraph, I see that I already have 2 articles called:

'Everything you need to know about Table Topics.'

'How to do a Toastmasters evaluation.'

So I can link those 2 **past** articles to the relevant keywords of my **present** blog post.

Okay.

Doesn't seem glamorous.

Correct, it doesn't seem glamorous.

But it's the concept that is money.

These 2 blogs I am linking are blogs that I wrote months back.

And yet, somehow they are connecting to the present.

The beauty of owning a blog is that it gives me a bird's eye view of how the mind works.

Information technology interests me because information technology is the mind in digital format.

And by seeing interconnections of the past to present, I am able to appreciate all experiences.

'All experiences? Come on man, we don't live in a fantasy land.'

Right, we don't.

'So you shouldn't be appreciative off ALL experiences. Some things would be better if it was avoided.'

That statement seems like a noble statement.

Yet, that's not how I view it.

It hasn't always been like this.
All experiences were welcomed with more open arms only when I saw interconnections happening in the outside world.
The blog being an example.

It takes 1 moment to make you think 'wait, I wonder if this experience will one day make sense.'

And when it does, that's when a deeper perspective is unlocked.

Matthew McConaughey was not only teaching his kids about delayed gratification that day.
He was also teaching his kids about building wealth.
And a little about farming.

Playing with time is a magical act.
It's something that everyone should experience first hand.

Difficult to explain.
Although it *can* be explained, it *should* to be an experience that is dealt with first hand.

Sort of like love.
Sort of like discipline.

It's no coincidence that great minds talk about delayed gratification.
"Delayed" is just a play on words for warping time.

IDEA MACHINE

My good friend **Abdul** recently gave me a shoutout on Twitter.
He is a large account who deals with financial mastery, online business & growth mindset.

In the shoutout, he gave me props for my consistency with this newsletter.

He joined this newsletter on 2019.
And he noticed that I write on it every day.
Haven't missed a day.

When he gave me the shoutout, I took some time to pause.
Yes, it has been daily for a large period of time.

When I first launched this newsletter, I did weekly emails.
Not daily.

And I would release it earlier on in the day.
So people could read it on their lunch breaks.

But after some time, I decided to go daily.

Daily didn't seem like a good idea.
Especially because it would mean a larger commitment.

However, for some reason, I thought about the commitment 2nd.
And the unsubscribers 3rd.

What I thought of 1st were the ideas.

After Abdul's shoutout, I went onto check that the streak had gone up to 784 days.

I had a teacher named Mr. Madigan for history.
He was this big, giant who looked like sasquatch.

In freshman year, he told our class:
'Enjoy high school. Because soon as you turn your head, the 4 years will be up.'

I thought, 'what a jackass!'
Does he really think 4 years are going to fly by?
Doesn't he know how much time that is?

He was right, and I was humbled.
4 years flew by.

I recall making this a daily newsletter after I came back from my brother's wedding.
It was a fun wedding in West Palm Beach.

After coming back, that's when the decision was solidified.

There were plenty of family and friends at the wedding who enjoyed my **best man speech.**

And a few of them pulled me aside and told me to take this seriously.
This thing with ArmaniTalks.

They didn't really know what sort of advice to give.
Because it was a different kind of business than they were used to.
It was a storytelling business.

But plenty of them were like, *'you got some raw talent. Keep working.'*

I didn't need encouragement to continue.
I would have done it regardless.

However, I thought getting extra pats on the back equaled a sign.

In the Bengali community, 2 professions are viewed with prestige
Engineers & doctors.

Other fields are seen as distant runner ups.

But when I saw a few doctors & engineers from the audience
coming to me after a speech and being like, *keep doubling down,*
I thought it was some sign.

One of the things I learned is that ideas comes to those who invest in ideas.

It's a game of constantly polishing up and maintaining a curious
attitude.

There is a tool on YouTube called Tubebuddy.
It's a tool that you can use to see what other people are searching
for.
Like what kind of keywords.

They have a "trending section."
Make a video on this and it will do great! they say.

I look at the trending topics.
It's talking about celebrity breakups, market crashes, politics etc.

All topics I believe that someone has a lane with.
However, it's not for me.

I try to cross combine ideas from different fields.
But the main part is <u>Armani</u>Talks.
The Armani part represents the experiences.

If it is outside the scope of my experiences, then it's not a topic I can talk about on a deep level for a story.

A cheatcode for infinite content is to factor in your experiences.
^Only a few people will take this line seriously.

'Why would I factor in my experiences?'
Because that's your unique advantage.
And that's the blueprint for telling your story.
Not someone else's.

It's also a key to finding inspiration anywhere you look.
And the key to becoming an idea machine.

Creativity follows vastly different rules than all other fields.
It's about being weird with structure.

Not weird on purpose.
When someone is weird on purpose, they become a try hard.

But weird by accident.
Great people are all weird by accident.

There's something about them that's different.

And that difference comes from them factoring their personality into the mix, somehow.

To become an idea machine, you have to see where you stand on issues.
But not the issues everyone else talks about.

On the contrary, issues that you experience first hand.
My formula for infinite content is to give advice to your younger self.

Because it gives you that 1 person to talk to.
And it collapses time.

When time is collapsed, ideas come at rapid rates.
Present you is going back to the past.
Past you is seeing the future.

Making a mockery out of time is how you make a mockery out of writer's block.

Writer's block is an illusion.
That's like saying you have walker's block.
You don't forget to walk because you always walk.

You forget to write because?
'Uh...'
Well, go on.'
'Because I don't always write.'
Correct.

So always write.
Be consistent.

Whether it's with twitter, or the pencil and paper.
It's a way to find out where you stand.
And be unique.

Be weird.
Just not the bad kind.

APOLOGIZE FOR SUCCESS?

You only see 1/9th of an iceberg.
The rest is submerged underwater.
Remember this part.

Around 2012 ish, it was Macklemore's era in terms of his genre of music.
Uplifting, ambitious anthems which could be played in any setting.
Him and his producer Ryan Lewis could do no wrong.

It was unpopular in my friend circle to say that you liked Macklemore.
They'd call you corny.

It was cool to say Drake, J Cole or Kendrick Lamar had great music.
But Macklemore?
Hell nah.

Well, I guess I was corny.

I'd been thru this before.
I used to love Backstreet Boys songs growing up.
But didn't want to be judged.
So would pretend like I didn't like their songs.

I wasn't going to repeat this again.
It was time to embrace what I liked.

Plus...
From the entire group, I was the only one with the car.

So the car holder got to decide which songs would get played.

Great memories.

It felt like Macklemore's rise was almost as quick as his decline.

There was one Grammy where everyone was expecting Kendrick Lamar to win the Album of the Year.

However, he didn't win.
Macklemore won.
And this shocked a lot of people.
Including Macklemore.

Just like that...
An upcoming artist who made great music was known as the symbol of white privilege.

To make matters worse, Macklemore sent a huge text to Kendrick saying how he was robbed, and screenshotted that text to post it on his IG.

Something about that felt abnormal.
It seemed like he was being a try hard.
And his fans let him know.

'Just accept the win & move on. You're coming off as corny.'
Notable music artists echoed similar sentiments.

You can make the argument that Macklemore was never the same.
It seemed like his ambition went away.
He was on top of the world and now he is being ridiculed for someone else's mistake?

The Grammy's.

What happens when someone is put in a situation like this artist?
Do they apologize?

It's easy to say, 'I would never apologize. I'm no bitch!'
But take some time to put yourself in his shoes.

He is an outlier in his field.
Not many rappers are white.
Although it may not seem like much from the outside...
Try to imagine how it will feel like from the inside.

Next, imagine you have a large publicity team all echoing different opinions at you.

Add in public distaste.
Then add in your character being questioned.

Now make the decision.
Do you apologize for your success or not?

I told you to remember something from the beginning.
The iceberg.
Only 1/9th is seen.

1/9th is the fame, the final product, the money.
But what is not seen?

The parts which are not seen include the constant stream of rejections, almost running out of money, sadness, joy, more sadness, battling writer's block, lost family time, being a poor friend, missed events, skipping out on meals, discipline, grit, cultivating ambition etc.

That's the part which is not seen.

When thinking about apologizing for your success...it's best to look at the part of the iceberg which is not seen, not the part which is seen.

Read the above line again.

The mind is a great area.

But leaving things in the mind allows things to get lost.

A process which is not acknowledged and remembered will be forgotten.

That's when one of the hardest worker's may fall victim to thinking that they were privileged.

I'm not saying Macklemore was the hardest worker.

I'm not saying Macklemore was not privileged.

I don't know anything about him other than his songs to be honest.

I'm talking about you.

The world around glorifies victimhood.

It can easily be seen as a badge of honor.

And to have victimhood, there needs to be an opposition.

Otherwise, the question would be....victim of what?

So the opposition is assigned.

The opposition are privileged people.

'Privileged people. But that's a vague phrase.'

Correct.

If you are rising up a field, others are not aware of your process.

Remember, I said most of the iceberg is under the water?

So what do you think others will view you as when you rise?

'Privileged?'

Correct.

'But I'm the last thing from privileged man! I work for mine every day.'

Everyday?

'Every day man!'

Oh well.

To others, the hard work will be underwater.

It's sad when your own hard work is under water even to you.

When faced with the question:

Do I apologize for my success?

Always recall the 8/9th, not the 1/9th.

The 8/9th will keep you humble.

The 8/9th will create more 1/9ths.

And the 8/9ths will give you better judgmental than a PR team ever will.

COINCIDENCES

I saw a very short, simple and profound tweet show up on my feed recently.

It was a tweet about God.

I don't recall the exact phrasing of the post.

But it went something like this:

'I believe in God for one simple reason. Coincidences. I don't know how you can be an Atheist and explain coincidences. We all had a few moments that shook us, don't lie....'

Can't recall the rest of the tweet.

I saw it as it was starting to pick up traction.

So don't know what the comment section looked like later on.

But when I did look at the initial comment section?

I saw a large group of people expressing support of the tweet.

They believed coincidences showed something deeper was going on.

I never heard the concept of coincidences bought up before when dealing with the bigger questions of life.

Even though it's not a stretch.

I'm just surprised that's not something I ever thought of.

Hey, you learn something new everyday, hopefully.

The reason why this tweet grabbed my attention was because of a coincidence I recently dealt with.

One of those coincidences which shook me.

In a good way though.

Recently, I was making a long drive.

And during the drive, I noticed my barber fucked up my haircut this time around.

Didn't like that.

My barber rarely messes up my hair.

This was one of the few times he wasn't on his A game.

'Was there any other times he messed up your hair?'

Yes...

I can recall the other time he messed up my hair because I had to shoot a YouTube video right after.

It was a video where I was wearing a *green* shirt.

It's a talk on 7 ways to learn storytelling.

Then I thought...

You know, the video where I am wearing a green shirt looks WAY different than the other YouTube video where I'm wearing a *black* shirt.

The video where I'm wearing a black shirt is a talk on fixing a monotone voice.

It's when my hair is long.

The green shirt video & black shirt video do not look like they were done by the same person.

In my world, the 2 Armani's look different.

They look like cousins, not the same person.

That's what I was thinking in the car ride.

Earlier this morning, I was adding some credit captions on my YouTube videos.

As I was doing it, I was letting a few of the videos play out to make sure the captions were working.

They were.

I have a feature on my YouTube videos where it recommends 2 suggested videos when the viewer reaches the end.

If the viewer does not click anything and remains on the screen, YouTube will automatically go to the next suggested video.

I was allowing the videos to continue until I got a call from a friend.

I answer the call.

The videos continue to play....

After the call is done, I come back to my laptop and see that there is a video of me with a GREEN shirt!

It was the video on 7 ways to learn storytelling.

'Wow, what a coincidence.'

No, that's not it.

YouTube also has a bar on the right that recommends other videos.

And guess what was the FIRST video recommendation?

'What?'

The video on how to fix a monotone voice!!

The talk where I'm wearing a black shirt.

When that happened, I was a little **spooked** out, not going to even front.

What are the chances of something like that happening?

A car ride where I pick 2 random video's on short hair vs long hair.

Then it just so happens that those videos randomly show up without me intentionally clicking on them??

Anyways, this talk is not about converting anyone.

I've had plenty of these random coincidences in my life.

And I'm sure you have too.

Often, I like to keep these coincidences to myself.

Helps me avoid too much bias.

I've come to see from personal experience that when the ego is untamed, people can use spirituality as a crutch to justify poor behavior.

To become extremely narcissistic.

Self love turns into love me, me, me.

It comes down to taming the ego.

Rather than putting yourself first... put yourself in context to the larger picture.

And understand your role in terms of the bigger picture.

I believe the bigger questions in life become more enjoyable to answer when narcissism can be tamed.

It's easy to fall into the egotistical path.

How can one curve it?

Simple....

Is your spirituality leading to benefits for anyone else other than yourself?

If the answer is no, then ego may be creeping up.

Coincidences mean different things to different people.
I'm sure I have a lot of Atheist & Agnostic readers.

And the point was not to convert anyone to a belief system.
I believe a belief system is best kept to yourself unless you get paid to debate on topics about it.
Or it needs to be said in a certain scenario.

What the point of this talk was to be open with spotting coincidences.

Because I don't know you.
And you don't know me.

But I'm sure both of us had plenty of coincidences which **shook** us to the core.

What does this 'shaking to the core' feeling imply?
It implies that no one has all the answers.
And life has a great way of making us humble.

It's as though nature had the *humble feature* designed into it's architecture.

Heartbreak and coincidences help bring us back to reality.
And coming back to reality is what prevents the mind from dreaming while awake.

LIFECYCLE OF AN IDEA

'Why do I get such general responses?'
Because you ask general questions.

I'll give you an example of a general question:
-How do I improve my communication skills?

Fam, Idk.
That's like asking, how do I get better at sports?

Which sport?
What move are you trying to get better at?
How long are you willing to dedicate?

But I don't want to be that guy.
The guy who asks a question with more questions.

The initial question about how to improve communication skills
was poor because it does YOU a disservice.

Let's say you are a great listener, know how to build rapport, text
on time.
But you mumble.

Is it fair to paint you as a poor communicator?
Not really.
Just 1 facet could be improved.
There are a lot of other facets that you are already good at!

By getting a tad bit more specific, the beast turns into a cute little
puppy.

A puppy who you can work with rather than a beast who you have to fight with.

It's the same concept with ideas.
Ideas can be broken down into a simple lifecycle.

1. Idea Connection
2. Idea Creation
3. Idea Expression

Idea connection happens with experiences and theory.
I wrote experiences before theory so introspection is leveraged before reading and learning from others.

By leading with introspection, it's easier to connect other ideas well.
And it'll stick out because our body is involved.

Experiences are stored in our body & true knowledge requires the body to be engaged just as much as the mind.

Idea connection leads to idea creation.
The random light bulb moment which comes from thin air mainly happens in cartoons.

And don't worry, I'm going to give you a live demo shortly.

The final part is idea expression.
This is when you share the idea with at least 1 person.
Either through writing or speaking.

To give you an example of this, let me take you down memory lane.

A couple of years back, I struggled with speech anxiety.
Hated giving speeches.

Noticed right before a speech, my heart would beat fast.

I spoke in the beginning with a rapid heart.
And this would alter my voice.
Didn't like that.

How can I fix this shaky voice?

A few weeks passed by and I was in the gym, running.
As I was running, I got a call.

Once I answered the call, my heart was beating rapidly.
But my voice?
Steady and in control.

What gives??

How come the rapid heartbeat before a speech caused an issue for my voice, but not the rapid heartbeat while on the treadmill?

I know why.
It's because I EXPECTED a rapid heartbeat for the treadmill.

Each time I was about to get on stage, I wasn't expecting the heart to move fast.
No clue why.
You would think a little common sense would have told my younger self to expect it.

But nope.

That gym session was the first day I had my aha moment.

After that aha moment, I got slick with it.
Anytime I was supposed to practice a speech, I would do pushups before hand.

I wanted to simulate the rapid heart beat, then give the speech.
And push through it anyways.

This forced me to control the breath.
But more importantly, it allowed me to EXPECT the heartbeat way before I got on stage.

Officially, the 'pushup to conquer speech anxiety' idea was born.

Once I saw this idea working multiple times, I decided to share the trick with my Toastmasters mentee down the line.
It worked for him.
He shared it with his mentee down the line.

And after it worked on a few more people, I made a YouTube video on the idea and gave it as a tip to my clients.

So, this was a simulation of idea connection, creation and expression.

I noticed a personal problem of the rapid heart beat.
A **connection** was made with public speaking and fitness.

The cross combination of the connection lead to the **creation** of an idea.

And the creation of the idea was **expressed** time and time again afterwards to help others with the same issue.

Don't want to be the bearer of bad news.
But ideas mean little if:
-it does not resonate with personal experiences.
-it is never shared.

For the first one, personal experiences.
Why is this so crucial?

It prevents you from being a fake smart guy.

Ever seen a fake tough guy?
Talks a bunch of shit behind the screen, but doesn't fight when met in person.

The fake smart guy is like that.
Knows a bunch, but can't do much with it.
Having personalized information side steps this issue.

Next, having all the ideas and keeping it to yourself because you're:
-selfish
or
-scared to share it
or
-unable to gather focus long enough to share it..

is still suboptimal.
The lifecycle of the idea has not been complete.

3 steps, my friend.
Idea connection.
Idea creation.
Idea expression.

If you struggle with ideas, don't ask a general question like:
-Why can't I ever get good ideas?

Instead, zone in!
Do you have a problem with connection, creation or expression?

And play around with the variable from there.
This gives hyper targeted responses for hyper targeted questions.

WORD OF MOUTH

I went to a small cruise in the beginning of this year.
One of my friends was going to propose to his girlfriend.
Let's call him Ben.

There were a lot of protocols involved.
Wear a mask.
Stay in a certain part of the boat.
And don't touch the rails.

To take it a level further, it began raining.
And raining bad.

The captain came to Ben and told him that he didn't know if we were going to be able to sail.
The cruise wasn't supposed to take too long.
Just a few laps around downtown Tampa.

This was going to throw off the plans.
Ben asked me and a few of his other friends what he should do?

All of us just said, *forget the cruise.*
Let's just chill inside even when the ship is docked.
Better than not boarding the ship at all.

Ben agreed.

1 hour passes by.

And Ben's girlfriend is accompanied by her friends to the cruise.
Ben's girlfriend had no clue what was about to happen.

She thought it was just a girls night out.

After coming in, Ben's girlfriend sees Ben.
He gives her a speech.
And then the proposal happens.

The other people in the ship were on the second story floor looking down.
There was this pathway which allowed us to see Ben and his girl.
Without his girl seeing us.
We were in stealth mode.

After she said yes, all the people in stealth mode started to celebrate.
This surprised Ben's girlfriend.
She saw her sisters, mom, dad, friends and a few relatives.

And guess what?

The rain had stopped.
The captain came and said we were good to begin the cruise!
That's when we sailed around Tampa.

This event was a tad bit awkward for me.
I knew Ben.
But I didn't know anyone else on the ship.
It was all his friends and his girlfriend's friends/relatives.

I sparked up a conversation with a few of them.
But things seemed dry.

A lot of the people were way older than me, or way younger than me, or couldn't speak English too well.

Eventually, I found 1 person to talk to.
He was a kid around my age who owned a chain of gas stations.
We talked business.

As the cruise went on...
An uncle walked towards me.

This man was 5'3.
Bald.
Smelled like vodka.
And was Bengali.

Then he looked up at me and said:
'I know you!'

I looked around.
But he poked his index finger on my chest.
'No, you. I know you. What is your name?'

I thought he was drunk.
I've never met this man in my life.
But I played along anyways.

I'm Arman.
And he says, 'no, you're Armani, right?'

Yes, I go by that too. How did you know?
That's when he said he'll be right back.
He leaves.

I thought that was strange.
Who was this uncle?

Then this man comes back with a picture on his phone.
'Look!' he said enthusiastically.

And it was a picture of a girl's hand holding my Level Up
Mentality book.
She was showing the back side of the book where my face is
shown with my arms crossed.

'Isn't this you?' he asked.
I said, *yes, that's me.*
I was happy that he bought the book and recognized me.

Then he bought it to my attention that he didn't buy the book.
His daughter did.
But he read it because she left it in the kitchen.

That was so random.
This drunk uncle was a very rich man in West Palm Beach.
Owned a bunch of gas stations.

Him and I immediately started talking.
He also didn't know anyone in the cruise.

What I noticed from this interaction was how word of mouth can
happen in a variety of ways.

Most of my readers are men.
But a lot of readers are now women as well.
Not a 50/50 split.
But it's more 50/50 than a lot of other writers.

So I found it compelling that his daughter found my book.
What made it more unique was that the book served as a
rapport building tool.

It was a conversation starter and a conversation keeper.

Plenty of people have great experience.
They want to compress their ideas and articulate it.
But they have no clue where to begin.

One service I began offering when I started ArmaniTalks was helping people write their first ever book.
And this uncle was considering it.

I don't know if it was the alcohol talking.
Or if it was the desire talking.
But he seemed very adamant about staying in touch to write a book.

We did stay in touch.
And he sent a couple of referrals my way after our interaction.
Plus, he taught me a lesson.

Content plays by a different rule than physical laws.
And content plays by a lot of the same rules as well.

The same rule comes down to a piece of content serving as an employee.
A brand ambassador.

And this ambassador works for you even when you are not physically present.

The different rule from the physical law is what I just stated above.
You don't need to be physically there.

But then again, all word of mouth is like that.

It's what they say when you leave the room.

Eventually, the person who is referring you even leaves the room.
Guess what though?
'What?'
The content piece can still stay in the room.
And an example was the book.

What does this all mean for you?
It may not mean much.
Or it can mean a lot.

Maybe you never want to write a book.
Or start a YouTube channel.
But maybe one day, you might...

And even if you know 100% that you aren't going to create any form of content.
That's fine.
But creating content is not always active.
It can also be passive.

-Active content is writing a book, blog, tweet etc.
-Passive content is building rapport, giving a strategic compliment by accident, being attractive.

Passive content happens by accident.
All content comes down to structured thoughts.

Word of mouth is simply a derivative.
What someone says about you is what they feel about themselves and the holistic feelings that they associated with you.

A certain segment of the population will always choose paper and pencil to write their journal rather than Microsoft Document.

A certain segment of the population will always choose paperback books over Kindle books.

Paper and pencil, physical book go beyond trends.

Likewise, same with referral marketing.
Facebook ads will come.
Instagram ads will come.
Snail mail will come.

But word of mouth is a sleeper pick.
Leave people better off than you found them.
And you may be surprised when you least expect it.

TONALITY

I used to have this very bipolar teacher named Ms. Waks.
She was my chemistry teacher.

When she was in a good mood, she was one of my favorite
teachers.
Probably top 2.

When she was in a bad mood, all the kids hated her.

To get on her good side, it was wise to tell her how she was losing
weight.
That was her sweet spot.

She was in a competition with another teacher on the floor to see
who was progressing better in their weight loss journey.
And the compliments made Ms. Waks feel more motivated.

There was one day when all the students were hyping her up.
And she was in a good mood.

Ms. Waks decided not to give us any classwork.
And we could just spend the rest of the class winding down.
Excellent.

Somewhere in the class session, there was a classmate named
Megan Baker who started a conversation with Ms. Waks.

I was sitting all the way at the right side of the classroom.
And Megan was sitting right by me.

Ms. Waks and Megan were talking.

Chatting away.

Somewhere in the conversation, Ms. Waks's dating life came up.
She would normally openly discuss her dating life.

I think she was the only teacher on the floor who had never been married.

Megan jokingly asked Ms. Waks when was the last time she went on a date.
And Ms. Waks said, *not for a couple of months.*

Suddenly, Megan in an **abrupt tone** says, 'LIAR.'

A lot of the kids from the right side of the classroom heard Megan's statement.
But the left side of the room didn't hear.

When Megan called Ms. Waks a liar like that, tides had shifted.
And Ms. Waks's dark side was about to come out.

'Don't call me a liar Megan. If I told you I haven't been on a date, then I haven't been on a date. But don't ever call me a liar like that again. Everyone, back to their seats. You can blame Megan.'

Ms. Waks called off this hangout session and gave us a chemistry lecture.

It wasn't what Megan said that day.
It was the **abrupt tone** that she said her statement in.

That 'Liar' remark could have easily been played off as a joke.
Ms. Waks would have remained in a good mood.

But no.

The abrupt, sharp tonality that Megan delivered the remark with altered Ms. Waks's behavior.

That's the power of tonality.

It has the power to build relationships.

Or burn bridges.

The sad part is that many individuals who have a poor tonality have no clue.

And some can't help it.

Their voice hurts when going to another cord.

The goal is to open up the ears first.

Observe tones that you enjoy.

And make a note of tones that you don't enjoy.

But it doesn't just stop with the ears.

It starts with the ears and goes to the body.

I'm sure when Megan called Ms. Waks a liar like that....Ms. Waks **felt it** in her body.

That's what tonality can do.

When you hear a tone, allow it to go in to the ears.

But the next questions are:

How does it make your body feel?

Pleasant or drained?

Smart people can have a tough time doing this because it seems counterintuitive.

We were graded for grammar, spelling and word usage.

When was tonality in the curriculum??
I don't remember having a tonality section on the SAT!

Because there wasn't a tonality section.
But the SAT section of **real world** has a tonality section.
It definitely does.

Are you passing with flying colors?
Or are you failing like Megan?

Damn Megan.
We were almost done with class too.
You just had to deliver the 'Liar' in a nicer way.

SIGNIFICANT CHANGES

There are 2 types of changes.
Change that someone begins, half asses, and stops.
Change that someone commits too.

The latter is often bought through focus on the details.
And the focus on the details is bought through heightened awareness.

What causes his heightened awareness?
Let me tell you a little story...

A couple of years back, it was pouring.
It was raining bad!
I think a hurricane was headed towards Florida.
Roughly around 2011.

I was stuck in my car parking lot for 40 minutes.
Was waiting for it to cool down so I could run to my apartment.

Eventually, the rain does settle down.
And I run into my apartment.

By the time I walk into my room, I became very disheartened.
'Why?'
My laptop was destroyed.

A bunch of the rain went through the window and demolished my laptop.
My desk was wet.
And all the papers were wet too.

No way could this laptop be fixed.
A new one needed to be purchased.

But I didn't have money to afford a laptop back then.
Was a broke college kid at the time.

I knew that my laptop being ruined would mean that I would
need to keep going to the school library to rent out their laptop.
This sucked.

Fast forward back to the present day.
I believe this was a few weeks ago.

I accidentally dropped water on my laptop.
Not just a little.
But a lot of water.

The flashback of my laptop being destroyed from years before
came flashing before me.
No!!!

I dried it up asap.
And awaited to see what would happen next.

'What happened next?'
The laptop was fine.

No damage whatsoever.
Worked perfectly!

Okay, lesson learned.
Keep water far away from my device.

No need to take the risk.

But something felt like the situation went too smoothly.
Felt like something bad was coming.

2 days ago, I am editing a Word document.
I got a ton of work done.
Almost about to wrap it up.

I try clicking on the buttons on the laptop...
And nothing is typing.

I restart it.
Reopen the document.
Start clicking on the buttons.
And nothing is typing.

Then immediately, the memory of me dropping all that water on my laptop flashed before my very eyes.
No!!

During the moment of restarting, I was very sad.
Just got this laptop recently, and it was perfect.
Great size, long lasting battery & easy to use.

I **really** did not want to buy another one.

If my troubleshooting was a success, I made a promise to take more care of this laptop.
Going to polish it and everything.

After the 6th time of restarting it...
Suddenly things changed.

The reason it wasn't working was because I missed the last software update.

After the update was installed....

The buttons began working again!

Since that moment, I built a **heightened awareness** to my laptop.

Whether it's with a software update.

Whether there is water near it.

Or anything that I'd consider funny business.

And this is how change often occurs.

During the valleys, not the peaks.

When my laptop was working fine, I didn't really care for it that much.

Not like I was intentionally harming it.

I just wasn't going out of my way to take extra care of it.

Picture that item in your house that is just there.

Let's say a toothbrush.

You probably understand the utility of it.

But you probably don't ponder much about what life will be like without a toothbrush.

The first time when all that water destroyed my laptop a couple of years ago...

That's when pain began.

-Every time I needed to use a computer, I had to take a bus to school. The bus ride took 15 minutes with all the stops included.

-Rent the library's laptop.

-Every now and then like an idiot, I'd forget my student card. Had to go back to my apartment to get it.

-Come back to the library.

-Rent out their laptop for 45 minutes.

-After the 45 minutes were up, I'd have to return it and get a new one.

Rinse and repeat.

Once I saw what a pain in the ass it was, I built a heightened awareness of never letting digital tools that I NEED anywhere near a window.
Florida has a lot of bipolar weather.

The good news is that circumstances can usually be reframed.

When someone wins, they win.
But when someone loses, they build the opportunity for heightened awareness.

That's when little details are noticed.
And that's when significant changes are made.
Not temporary ones.

CONFIDENCE

A few years back, I was walking in the Tampa International mall with a few friends.

As I was walking, I noticed 2 very tall blonde women walk right past me.
They looked very familiar.

As I was trying to recall who the 2 were, one of my friends shouts out:
'Yo, that's Brooke Hogan!!'

Brooke Hogan is Hulk Hogan's daughter.
Hulk Hogan was a wrestling icon in the 80s and 90s.

And during the time of this story, the reality show, **Hogan Knows Best,** was blowing up.
It was a very popular show on VH1.

'Armani, you mentioned there were 2 blondes. Who was the other blonde with Brooke?'
That was Hulk Hogan's girlfriend.

Around that time, Hulk had just gone through a public divorce.
What made it strange was that the girl he dated next ended up looking just like his daughter.
This set the media on a frenzy!

As Brooke Hogan and Hulk Hogan's girlfriend walked past me, my friends were plotting their next moves.
Should we get a picture with them or not?

The friend group consisted of 4 other people.
And these were bold folks.
They already had their mind made up.
Which caused me to have my mind made up.

Let's get this damn picture.

We all walked into the Burberry store & asked Brooke for a picture.
She was sitting on the couch.
Brooke agreed to take a picture with each one of us.

I'm 6 foot tall.
But as I sat next to her, we almost were the same size.
She was huge.

There was another friend with me who I'm going to call Asif for the sake of the story.
He was 5'4.
Asif also got a picture with her.

Once we all got our pictures, we thanked Brooke, congratulated her on the success of her show, then went about our day.

Later on in the evening, I posted my picture on Facebook.
Asif did the same.

A few hours went by...

As the few hours went by, my picture got some comments.

But Asif's picture was BLOWING UP!

Not in a good way though.

Most of the people commenting on his picture were making fun of him.
His height disparity with Brooke was very noticeable in the image.
He looked like a child next to her.

Some of the comments went like:
'You're so tiny bro!'
'You should sit on her lap, little man.'
'You look like a Teletubby!'

People were making fun of him nonstop.
After 1 more hour of the harassment, Asif ended up taking the picture down.

He had bent the knee.
Not to the social media mob.
Instead, to the harassment of jokes.

'Do you think Asif made the right choice?'
I can't quite say.

Because for a long period of my life, I was not the tallest. I was the shortest kid in my class.
It wasn't until 11th grade till I had my growth spurt from 5'3 to 6'0.

Getting mocked for being short was not something that Asif only felt in his life.
I felt it as well.

So I couldn't quite say what I would of done.
Or if he was wrong.

What I did notice is that different people handle shortness in different ways.
-Some power up.
-Some power down.

I know this one guy who has a beard & is very short.
He says that the beard helps him get dates.
However, his height hurts him.

He has grown a resentful attitude regarding his height over the years.
He even introduced me to a phrase called **heightism**.

'Armani, you know a lot of girls are heightists, right?' he asked in indignation.
What the fuck is that??
'That's when they discriminate you for being shorter than 6 foot' he responded.

He grew resentful of the discrimination he faced for something he couldn't control.

On the other hand, I know another kid who is VERY short.
He was on a reality dating show recently.
And he ended up going much further in the competition than a lot of people expected solely due to his humor.

He doesn't wear his height with disgrace.
Instead, he doesn't wear it at all.
It's a part of him.

But he brings other things to the table.

There's a big difference between handsome and attractive.
Handsome is physical.
Attractive is mental.

There is a big difference between hot & beauty.
Hot is physical.
Beauty is mental.

This is what confidence is about.
-Not dwelling on what you can't control.
-But doubling down on what you can control.
-So what you can't control isn't that big of a deal.

Growing overly resentful gives the illusion of progress.
While in reality, no progress is being made.

It's a case of the man in the quick sand moving more, digging himself deeper into the quicksand.

When faced with certain setbacks beyond your control, you should stop & see which attributes you **can** control.

Qualities like storytelling, humor, explaining things with clarity can be done by anyone.
Doesn't matter your height, gender or religion.
Try focusing on these traits.

Confidence is a game of constant redirecting.
After constant redirecting, the mind becomes fixed in the position you initially intended to set it on.
That's working with what you have.
Rather than crying over what you don't' have.

SIMPLY SIMPLE

Yesterday, I talked about a few ways to build confidence if you consider yourself ugly.

A few things I recommended were to improve storytelling skills, humor and the ability to explain things clearly.

Let me zone in on the final one for todays email.

The ability to clearly explain something.

To do anything clearly, the methods must be made simple.

And the delivery must be made even simpler.

I'm not sure how long you have been on this newsletter.

But most of the topics I discuss are designed in a way where a 4 year old can read it.

At times, this may make me seem like a very silly fellow.

Most likely someone who isn't smart.

What kind of smart person talks like a 4 year old?

^That's immediately how plenty of people's mind operates.

That's the nature of the game.

Plenty of people who write & speak in simple terms are perceived as not being smart.

This dilemma is what kills simple communicators.

They worry over perception.

Imagine this scenario....

You have spent years training to be an engineer.

Went to school for it, got internships on it & dedicated the last 15 years of your career on it.

One day, a teenager comes to you and asks what you do for a living.
And you proceed to explain your career in very **simple** terms.

After hearing your talk, the teenager's eyes light up:.
'That's it?? I guess anyone can be an engineer!'

You are livid.

The clear explanation gave this poor fool the illusion that what you do for a living is not difficult.
Being an engineer is one of the hardest fields out there.

Now this teenager is going around to his friend circle parroting what you just said, acting like they are the subject matter expert.

The next time a different teenager comes to you asking what you do for a living....**you make it extra complex.**
You don't want what happened last time happening again.

This is pride.
And that pride kills clear communicators.

'Wait a minute man. Why would I want to speak simple if I'm perceived as basic?'
I never said everyone perceives you as basic.
I said *some* people may.

For the most part, people listen to simple speakers who deliver knowledge with a sense of gratitude.

When you can turn a complex subject into a simple one, people with skin in the game will know that you mean business.

People without skin in the game will listen to you with more curiosity vs the guy who sounds like he is reading off a dictionary.

Simple speaking is like getting a 6 pack.

Sure, Javier wants a 6 pack.
But it's not going to be attained by simply wanting it.
The 6 pack requires effort.

Same with simple speaking.
Everyone wants it.
Even people who don't understand its hidden brilliance.
But only a few people will work for it.

I recommend journaling, getting in the habit of articulating ideas by starting a YouTube channel or some form of practice.

How about this:
Find the most complex topic you know and explain it in 30 seconds.

Don't speed through your words.
Maintain the speed that you normally speak in.

Then explain in 30 seconds.
This forces you to chop off extra words.

And by a complex topic, I mean any topic you know very well.
We all have a subject like that.

It can be cooking, basketball, Microsoft Excel etc.

Just explain the basic fundamentals and what is required to succeed in that field.

If you go over 30 seconds, that's fine.
Try again.
And again...
And again.....

If you can do it in 30 seconds with ease, then cut it down to 15 seconds.

You may feel sharp stinging sensations in the head area.
Don't panic.
That's your neural pathways rewiring itself to get to the point.

Simple speaking looks easy from the outside.
However, when you try it out for yourself, it's not that easy.
It's a workout for your speech, the mind & persuasion skills.

This is just one of many ways to build confidence & add value.
Especially if you consider yourself to be ugly .

TELLING YOUR STORY

It's a busy world out there.
Learn to get to the point.

And it's not just about getting to the point.
It's about telling your story.

I had a great podcast with LifeMathMoney recently which went up to almost 3 hours.
For 3 hour long podcasts, it's best if there are some time stamps on it.

So I listened to it before releasing it to put some time stamps in each segment.
That got me familiarized with the interview.

When you actively put timestamps on something, your mind goes from seeing a book to seeing the chapters.

What was initially a 3 hour interview now turned into segments.

As I continued labeling, I noticed the transitions in topics.
We went from talking about social media censorship all the way to masculine/feminine energy.

Huh??
Where's the correlation in that?

Then there was a segment on perfectionism all the way to discussing the role of anger in human life.

Huh??

Where's the correlation in that?

As I was going through this podcast, I made a stunning parallel into another world.

'What world was that?'

Anthologies.

I'm currently working on a short story collection called Word Play.

Be on the lookout for that.

It's a collection of 101 short stories, essays and insights to improve communication skills.

As I was creating it, I notice how different the topics were.

The titles seemed so different from one another.

Sort of like how different the chapters were in this podcast interview.

While working on the book, I decided to check out Amazon to see if more people sold short stories.

The more I looked, the more I couldn't quite find what I was looking for.

There were many sellers who **literally** sold short stories.

A book that was only 50 pages.

But that's not what I meant.

I was looking for other sellers who sold a COLLECTION of short stories.

Because Word Play is couple hundreds of pages, not 50 pages.

After looking for a while, I noticed I kept coming across the phrase **Anthology**.

Anthology?
What the fuck is an anthology??
That's definitely not what I am looking for!

Or is it?
Did Word Play somehow turn into an anthology book?

After Googling the definition, my mind was blown.

-An anthology is a collection of ideas and stories with a shared theme and/or author.

That's exactly what I was looking for!
And that's pretty much what the podcast came out too as well.

The topics seem very disparate from one another.
But when looking closer, all the topics relate to self improvement in some way shape or form.

LifeMathMoney discusses self improvement thru the topics of finance, habits and discipline.
I discuss self improvement thru the topics of communication skills.

That's what served as the thread of unity underlying the disparity.

'How does this all relate to telling my story?'
It helps make the process easier.

Let's say you want to make the remaining of 2021 the year where you become a better storyteller.

Something about storytelling resonated with you.
-Maybe you want to learn it for fun.

-Maybe you have to learn it for your job.
-Or maybe you want to learn it just to see what it's about.

Your mind may trick you into overloading in the beginning.
Trying to craft grand tales from scratch.

Like telling a 30 minute story.
Or wanting to immediately write a book.

That's when you want to take a step back and start off light.
Try telling short stories.

It can be a few sentences long.
Or a few minutes long.
But start off light.
Train your mind to think like that.

You may notice 1 story is about dogs.
While another story is about your earliest childhood memory.

Then you may be like....
What do dogs and my childhood memory have in common?

YOU.
That's what all your stories have in common.
The storyteller.

An anthology is a collection of stories that shares the same author or theme.
Start off with anthologies before you try doing something grand.

The podcast we did was 3 hours long.
And that's how most listeners probably saw it.

But I saw it as 65ish tiny short stories about different topics.

By changing the mind from seeing a big 3 hours to a tiny 65...
You go from a gargantuan ship to a tiny speedboat mentality.

Sure, the ship is big.
However, the speedboat is **dynamic**.
The speedboat allows for more creativity.
And not too much commitment is needed.

When you're first learning a topic, play around a little to get a feel for it.
That's what it's like with short stories.

Experiment with different topics.
See which resonate with you.
Allow completely different topics to show up.

At the end of the day, it'll always be the same storyteller.
That's what these tiny tales which seem so different have in common.

Tell more tiny tales in a world where concentration levels are plummeting.
Eventually, these tiny tales will start to feel like tiny people.

Check out my free masterclass on how to tell short stories for beginners. Normally, it's a paid class.
However, whoever joins from this link will access it for free.

STREET SMART FOR LIFE

I made a video a while back regarding street smarts on YouTube.

Recently, I found out it was ranking for a specific key word.

This led people from the YouTube ecosystem to discover the ArmaniTalks brand.

One of the guys who watched the video followed the trails and discovered my Twitter.

He messaged me and said *'yo man, your video on street smarts was funny!'*

Funny?

Then he went onto say *'I had the same thing happen to me.'*

You may be wondering what that **thing** is.

It's the thing of beef stew.

The street smarts video talked about how we never fully know what to expect.

That's why I believe application is better than theory for learning.

Theory is needed.

But in my lens, application is more important.

In the video, I talk about creating beef stew for the first time.

Initially, when I made it....it tasted awful!

Made me want to throw up.

What happened?

I followed the recipe to the tee.

Why did it taste so bad for?

I tried making it again....
And once again, it tasted awful!

It took me 7 tries of failing to start noticing a pattern.
'What was the pattern?'
The beef was chewy.

I knew it tasted bad before, but couldn't explain why.
I just said 'ew' and threw it away.

So the beef is too chewy...
Now we are getting somewhere.

Eventually, I found a cooking forum that was talking about fixes
for the predicament I was in.

*When your beef is chewy, that means you forgot the vinegar or
you didn't allow the meat to cook long enough.*

Vinegar's acid helps break the meat down.
Cooking the beef longer allows the meat to become tender.

I tried it.
Will the 8th time be a charm?

It was!

I made the mistake of trying to cook beef like chicken.
This moment was street smarts calling my name.

I looked at the recipe many times before attempting to cook the dish.

Never could I have predicted that chewy beef was going to be a problem.

It only became a problem when I started cooking.

That's why the guy who messaged me was excited to let me know that he had the **same exact** issue.

You'll see when someone knows a topic, they speak in a targeted way.

They'll notice things that someone who is only familiar with the theory will not notice.

People with street smarts have more empathy too in my opinion.

Because they know the answer is not always that simple.

It's easy to give black and white advice nowadays:

Never have fun.

Always hustle.

Only hang with people who want to be a billionaire.

Yes, all that is good in theory.

But in practice, different pain points arise.

That's why I'm not a big fan of 50/50 anything.

That's theory talk trying to enter the real world talk.

Is anything purely 50/50?

Not really.

Street smarts does not get rid of book smarts.

It just shows what's more important in my opinion.

I said nothing is 50/50.

Then what is it?

1 side leads and the other side magnifies.

Street smart leads and book smarts magnifies.

So rather than reading books for the sake of reading books, it's now a game of reading books for a purpose.

If you saw me just reading recipe book after recipe book, with o desire to cook a single dish, you'd think *'what a wierdo! Who acts like that?'*

However, plenty of people are acting like that with their modern content consumption.

As the famous saying goes:

-Knowledge without application is philosophy.

-Application without knowledge is ignorance.

Use both.

But when it's all said and done, you'll notice 1 side is always leading a bit more than the other side.

PRIMAL CONNECTION

A couple of years back, I had a white friend named Toby in my masters class with me.

Why I bought up his skin color will make more sense shortly.

I was happy to have Toby in grad school with me because I knew him in undergrad.

I was a full time employee then and I didn't know how much effort I could give to this program.

Toby was luckily a part time employee and a fulltime student.

There was a level of comfort knowing that he could give me updates, and connect me with the right people if need be.

Due to my busy schedule, I knew some of the other students in the curriculum, but was not close enough to call any of them a friend.

We all just sort of knew each other.

Toby was the one who tried to be very close with everyone.

However, something peculiar happened.

'What?'

I was the one getting invited to the 'exclusive' study sessions.

The program I was in was 85% Desi people. People from the South Asian area.

A few of the leaders of the groups (the most social ones) would invite others to the exclusive study sessions.

Which were the sessions that were hosted in someone's house and not the library.

These sessions were a blend of a party vibe with study vibe.

It's where in depth knowledge was dropped.
This knowledge would skyrocket the learning curve of the class.

Some of these people would randomly add me on Facebook to extend the invite.
Some would directly ask me in class.
Others would chase me down as I was going to my car in the parking lot.

My question was...why the hell was I getting invited?
I barely knew some of these people.

It didn't matter.
A large reason why was because I looked like them.
Toby did not.

This wasn't something I would say was malicious.
It was more so of keeping it culture based.

Whenever I asked if I could bring Toby too, they would say 'Sure man. Bring him as well!'

It's not like they were excluding Toby intentionally, it's more so that they didn't even consider to ask him.

They thought he would be studying with the white students.
Just like a lot of the Chinese students studied with the Chinese Students.
And a lot of the Egyptians studied with the Egyptians.

That's one thing I found very unique about post grad.

Where there was more freedom to let students study how they wanted to study....

There were **specific** situations that happened and **generalized** situations that happened.

The specific situation was a guy like me and Toby hanging out.

I never even viewed us as being different cultures like that. Neither did he view it like that for me.

For both of us, we viewed each other as a familiar face from undergrad.

That was our shared connection.

Note: We knew each other before.

But for a lot of the other people in the curriculum?

Some knew each other before hand.

However, many didn't.

So when left to form groups, they immediately drifted to who LOOKED familiar.

This is why I am very aware of skin color and physical looks in terms of human dynamics.

Trying to push it to the side completely is a noble wish.

Even if you don't view skin color and physical looks as a factor in your day to day experience, understand other people may.

It's not always looks that form a hidden connection.

Sometimes, it's a degree.

A shared organization joined.

Job profession that you escaped.

I was living in New Jersey for a while.

One day, in the metro, I saw this guy warning a silver band on his pinky ring.

Immediately, in a rapid impulse, I'm like 'Did you graduate from the college of engineering??'

He enthusiastically said yes and we talked like we were lifelong friends.

The silver band ring is given when you graduate from that college..

A bond was instantaneously formed.

No need for rapport building and much small talk.

If you placed me and the guy from the metro in an environment where we knew no one, we would probably gravitate towards one another because of the rings.

When understanding dynamics, understand there is a place for logic.

But also understanding some things happen in a **primal manner.**

You don't need to agree with it.

You don't even want to be politically correct with this one.

Just observe *without* judgment.

When boundaries are stripped, how are people acting?

A mind filled with bias will never understand power, persuasion and how interactions work.

A mind that cuts back on bias is capable of seeing how, why and where people move.

They can look at the actions beyond the words.

YOU JUST NEVER KNOW

You know what I've always found strange?

'What?'

How people effortlessly create associations.

Let's say John's brother ends up killing someone.

People are going to be livid at John's brother.

Plus, many may be livid at John as well.

Some of them may be like:

'Well, John clearly knew his brother was a murderer. How couldn't he? I mean they were around each other for so long.'

I believe it was Nassim Taleb who bought up the concept of the Black Swan.

How a disparate data point can throw off EVERYTHING. Making future scenario's difficult to predict.

Likewise, social black swan's exist as well.

Yesterday, I told a story in my YouTube video about working in a driving company named Zingo with a guy named Terry.

In the video, I talked about how Terry was always tripling or quadrupling me in tip money.

Terry had the guts to start a conversation with the passenger's, while I didn't.

African American with a small afro, swag, and a sense of humor.

He taught me his ways by telling me to spark up some conversations as well.

We worked together for a few months as Zingo began to scale.

Eventually, a 40 year old named Trae was hired and another kid in his early 20s named Shane was hired.

After I stopped working in Zingo, I completely lost touch with Terry.

Clearly, we were just co workers and that was it.

I believe 2 years ago, when I was in some sort of reunion event, I came to find out Terry was in prison.

'Wait, forreal?? What did he do!'

Apparently, he had child pornography and got caught with it.

I don't know the details of the story.

But what I do know is that I saw his mugshot.

A sad face wondering how he could have thrown his life away.

If you were to ask my 20 year old self what I envisioned for Terry in the future, I'd actually say, **'big things.'**

His ability to effortlessly start conversations, dance, tell jokes made for an interesting personality.

However, the social black swan had completely changed my perception and his future.

It's something that was pretty shocking to be honest.

Yet, it gave me perspective of how people act heinous out of the blue moon.

There was a moment in Bangladesh a couple years ago when 4 college students had beheaded some people in a well known restaurant.

When looking at these 4 students, you'd never be able to predict that they would be capable of such a crime.

Baby faced assassins.

To make sense of the atrocity, that's when the mind goes to, *'oh, the parents must have known!'*

Did the murderers subconsciously pick up behaviors from their parents?

I literally have no clue so I'm not going to talk about that.

What I'm more curious about is why people from multiple parts of the world make the knee jerk response to seamlessly create associations before all information has been gathered.

Broadchurch is a British detective series where the show begins with a dead boy.

That's what starts the suspense of the show.

Everyone knows each other in this small city that Broadchurch is filmed in.

Who killed this boy?

Everyone looks at their neighbor with an eerie eye.

I'm going to give a spoiler by the way.

So if you plan to watch Broadchurch, apologies.

It's eventually discovered that the police chief's husband is the killer.

Just imagine.

The same police chief that is looking for the killer....

Is sharing a house with him.

Eventually, the parents of the murdered boy ostracize the police chief.

The community starts giving her the cold shoulder.

'How could she possibly not have known that her husband was capable of such an act?'

Dark truth?

We have 0 clue what someone is capable of.

We just make estimations to feel good about the uncertainty.

An association is simply the framework adopted to deal with that uncertainty.

When I say we have 0 clue what someone is capable of, it implies the good and the bad.

-Someone who you thought was going to do BIG things, may be convicted for murder in 7 years.

-Someone who you thought was going to be an average bubba shocks the world and becomes a billionaire. He or she was quiet, but was working very hard behind the scenes.

The point is to remain open minded and know that black swans in the social world exist.

It's the knee jerk response to blame others in close vicinity of those who committed the black swans, but I believe that judgment should be withheld for some time.

Understand this black swan.

Use this as a chance to learn about psychology.

Build understanding.

Know that nothing is fully finite in the world of the mind, emotions and human nature.

Things change.

Moods change.

Circumstances change.

Aim to stay clear sighted through all of that...

KAMIKAZE

Kamikaze is defined in a few different ways.

One definition is:

"An intentional suicide mission of crashing into the enemy target."

Another definition is:

"A person who behaves in a destructive manner."

Both definitions are not too different from one another.

But for the sake of this talk, I'm going to be focusing on the latter definition.

Kamikaze is a dangerous social move.

It's often done by someone who has **nothing** to lose.

Which is why it's smart to not burn bridges for no reason.

And why it's smart to not talk down on someone below you.

All this sounds great in theory.

But is there an example?

Sure.

I don't talk about popular culture much.

However, there have been a series of events recently that plugs in beautifully with the Kamikaze move.

Quick disclaimer.

This talk deals with a topic in the world of sports.

But you don't have to be a sports fan. Just stay aware of the names I use.

Around 2008ish, Los Angeles Lakers struck a mega deal to land Pau Gasol.

A star who guaranteed the Lakers a playoff run.

Guess who was traded?

'Who?'

A man named **Kwame Brown.**

Kwame up until that point was viewed as one of the biggest busts in NBA history.

And his name was tied with more infamy because the most renowned basketball player of all time, Michael Jordan, drafted him.

After Kwame was traded, a sports reporter named Stephen A Smith went on a tirade insulting Kwame.

Talking about why the city of Los Angeles should be celebrating his departure.

And mercilessly bashed Kwame.

That clip ended up going viral.

And ultimately, the tirade **destroyed** Kwame Brown's public perception.

Kwame was silent for years after that.

Years later, players, sports analysts and fans continued to throw dirt on Kwame's name.

They called him every name in the book.

Kwame was silent.

'Why wasn't he defending himself?'

Around 2008, players didn't have access to media like they do nowadays.

Back then, what ESPN said was law.
And Stephen a Smith was the brand ambassador.

After years of being silent.
Tides shifted.

As of late, Kwame Brown has been firing back at his critics.
Notable media members who have been disrespecting him are now getting a response.

And one of the members who got the brunt of his tirade was...
Can you guess?
'Stephen a Smith?'
You are correct.

Seeing Kwame go on these long live streams looks like a man who has nothing to lose.

A man who had his public perception destroyed and a less than stellar NBA career to show for it.
What does he have to lose?

At one moment, Kwame looks unhinged.
Dropping a ton of curse words, riding in a truck talking to a camera, bringing up players exe's, and calling his attackers every name in the book.

At the next moment, Kwame looks like a **comedian**.
'Comedian?'
Yes, a comedian.

I see him as funny.
Not the idiotic kind of funny acting like a clown.
I actually think he is very well thought out.

And his humor has been working as of late.

His YouTube channel yesterday morning had 20,000
subscribers.
And he ended the day with 40,000 subscribers.

The way he labels someone, makes it **stick**.
He called Stephen a Smith a <u>turtle without the shell.</u>

This is funny to me.
But what's funnier is the imagery he used.

He called one of his attackers Matt Barnes, <u>Becky with the Good
Hair.</u>
Which is a slang phrase taking away all of Matt Barnes street
cred.

He called another attacker Stephen Jackson, <u>a fake activist.</u>
A guy who wants to fight one day and march in protests the next.
Making Stephen Jackson look like a confused man.

All these attacks seem like jokes at first.
But I believe it's a great lesson on psychology.
Kwame is funny.
But he is funny with **intent**.

'Where do you think his humor came from?'
I think his humor came from pain.

By being the butt of all jokes, it's wise to learn to tell jokes.

Ask plenty of professional fighters WHY they became street fighters...
They will say, 'I got tired of getting bullied.'

Ask plenty of comedians WHY they became a comedian....
They will say, 'I got picked on. Didn't have much going on for me. But no one could do a better yo momma joke than me.'

A lot of comedians are born through pain and by being a laughingstock at one point or another.

2008 Kwame Brown was the laughingstock of the NBA.

It's all fun and games looking at it as a consumer of the media.
But it's different when you are viewing it from his life.

I don't know much about his personal life.
However, I think he has kids, parents and friends who are well aware of what a laughingstock he used to be.

He was silent for many years.
And I think being such a joke created a 'no fucks given' attitude.

It's impossible for a comedian to be optimal funny without a 'no fucks given' attitude.
Otherwise, they are too politically correct.

Along with Kwame's rants, there are sudden flashes of deep truths that are keeping people coming back to watch his channel.

He talks about the selective narratives that the mainstream media plays.

How they turn one against another.

How people of power strategically hire people to keep an agenda going.

At first glance, he seems to be losing it.

But for me, I think he's having his Kamikaze moment.

Other than the Kamikaze moment, the other communication lesson to learn from all of this is the power of new media.

A power many people take for granted.

Kwame insulting a media behemoth like Stephen a Smith would have been seen as blasphemy a couple of years back.

But strategical use of media technology can allow a node to topple the network.

If Kwame can work on his humor, and expand his content material, I can see him having a renaissance in his career.

It may be a large turnaround from 'being the biggest NBA draft bust of all time' to an 'athlete turned entertainer.'

Or maybe I'm completely wrong.

Maybe the buzz dies down within a few days and all else is back to normal.

That's definitely a possibility.

A few lessons in all of this:

1. You never know when someone can snap & pull a kamikaze.

2. Never underestimate the power of humor

3. Never underestimate strategic use of new media.

A combination of these 3 is allowing Kwame to have a strange resurgence in 2021.

And who knows how long this resurgence will last.

LEARNING FROM DEFEAT

I'm a big fan of the fight game.
I don't just watch how fighters take a win.
A bigger learning point is how they take a loss.

A while back, I began following this upcoming female fighter.
Let me call her Ashley for the rest of the email.

Ashley made a splash by going viral for a knockout punch last year.
That's how I became introduced to her.
Decided to follow her on Instagram to see her progress.

As the coming weeks went by, she began to have a polarized audience.
Plenty of people followed her for the fighting.
However, she seemed like she wanted to be an Instagram model as well.

That's when she received criticism for not focusing fully on her craft.
A part of her also wanted to explore boxing too!

A mixed martial artist who wanted to be an Instagram model and a boxer.
Hm...
Attention seems to be **split**.

The fight game doesn't lie.
Either you win or you lose.

I'm not too active on Instagram.

Due to my inactivity, I lost touch with this fighter's updates for a couple of months.

However, a couple of weeks ago, I heard she was going to be fighting.
Interesting...
What was going to happen??

I ended up getting pretty busy in her fight weekend, so didn't stay updated.

After the weekend was done, I saw a post that showed her knocking out her opponent.
I guess she won!
Good for her.

She had a long description on her post which I did not feel like reading.
So, I just kept on scrolling.

As some time went by, I saw another page report that Ashley had lost the fight.

Wait, what??
I just saw that she won.

I went back on her page and looked at the picture again.
Yes, she was knocking out her opponent.
Clearly, she won.

At this point, I was confused.
So I decided I was going to read this long ass paragraph that she wrote.

I read it...
And was a tad bit disappointed.
Ashley had lost.

I wasn't disappointed by her losing.
It was more so regarding the description.

The way the post was framed, it seemed like her opponent had gotten lucky.
Ashley framed herself as having been in the beginning of her career, so that's why this setback happened to her.

Was she in the beginning of her career?
Yes.
Was her opponent also in the beginning of her career?
Yes.
Was credit given to the opponent for winning?
Not quite.

This was a case of not taking a Loss with grace.

Losses happen to the best of us.
Especially in a sport like fighting. Where your ego can get heavily invested in the process.

I hated playing video games for that reason.
It's because I suck at that field. Any game. If it's multiplayer, I normally take the L.

This has me getting pissed off.
Especially at the person who beat me.
The last thing I want to do is shake their hand.
This was my past self.

I came to realize that losses happen in all facets of life. Ego hits come in **all** shapes and sizes.

Let's envision a guy named Nestor who has the safest job in the world.
He puts the cotton stuffing in the medicine containers.
Day in and day out.

Seems like a fairly safe job.
Well, when it's too safe, there's a guarantee an ego hit will happen in another form.
That's just how nature is programmed.
'For all of us?'
Yes, for all of us.

Maybe Nestor has an annoying boss.
This is one of those mean bosses that you see on TV shows.
Except in Nestor's situation, it's real life.

With social media, it's easy to run away from a Loss.
The way that Ashely created the post, it truly did seem like she won.
In her mind, I think she even convinced herself she won. She probably framed it like she was taken advantage of.

Information age is equivalent to the Instant Gratification age.
People want quick wins.
But they don't want to take slow losses.

Learn to take a loss like a champion by learning that you had the loss in the first place.
It's a game of acceptance being the king.

Who knows how Ashley's next fight will go.

Maybe she comes back with more hunger.

What I did notice is that a split attention does not produce greatness.
Especially in the beginning portions of a journey.

It's a game of getting that attention and harnessing it like a sun behind a magnifying glass.
Then creating the narrative, 'it's either greatness or bust.'
No balancing acts for a while.

Few take this path.
But those who do... definitely learned how to take a loss like a champion.
Make no mistake about that.

CHICKEN AND POTATOES

A few years back, I had this wealthy man in his 60s hit me up to help him with his speech.

In the beginning stages, it started off with a speech.

As more time went on by, he started asking me to help with his marriage and emotions.

When it started off with speeches, I felt comfortable working with him.

If it dealt with social skills, I could have worked with him too.

But hearing too many of the personal details with his marriage and giving him tips on that was not my lane.

I told him I could let him off our sessions early and he'd get our latest session for free.

It would have been easy to milk this situation.

Here is this wealthy man, emotionally volatile, willing to give me money for advice.

However, the advice I was being asked to give was not fully in alignment with my field of competence.

So, I turned the money down.

For some of the people reading this, they would think what I did was common sense.

While another group may be like, *'fuck that...I'd take the money! haha.'*

I've been a short term thinker before.

Nowadays, I'm team long term.

Actions steps I take are meant to benefit myself all the way up to 15 years from now.

That's how I like thinking.

Which is why telling this gentleman to seek professional help from a therapist was a high ROI move for me.

This man went onto give me plenty of referrals since that moment.

It's because he believed me to be a congruent person who doesn't take advantage of others.

Thus far since being in business, there has not been a single person that I'm aware of who said, *'Armani went out of his way to screw me over.'*

There are reviews on my site from notable brands, CEOs and presidents of companies.

I go out of my way to make sure someone wins before I get a penny out of them.

This is not too brag.

It's to bring a very simple formula into your consciousness.

Use value **before** cash value.

More on this shortly....

I used to be a big fan of fitness.

It was one of my first loves.

My younger self would spend my Dunkin Donuts money buying supplements, I'd read all the blogs and try all the unique workouts.

However, after some time, I started to fall out of love with it.
'Any idea why?'
Yes, because of analysis paralysis.

It was peculiar because I was a doer in so many parts of my life.
I was even a doer in fitness.
Yet, after some time, I started to get contradictory information in the fitness field.

There were 2 guys in my gym named Lane and Daniel.

Lane was a 6 foot white guy.
Daniel was a 6 foot Asian guy.

Both had a lot of muscle with low body fat.
I wanted a body like them...
When I approached them for advice, they gave **different** advice.

One was telling me just about keto.
The other kept saying become a vegetarian.
One was pro creatine.
The other one strongly advised against it.
This is just scratching the surface.

The 2 were going out of their way to convert me to their tribe.
It's like they would win another member over, and that was their main goal.
They rarely asked me what **my** goals were.

Recently, I conversed with 2 big fitness accounts on Twitter.
Once again...
2 individuals with physiques that I admired.

I decided I was going to ask them some questions so they can clear up the fitness contradictions.

As I asked them, I had some fear in the back of my mind.

The memories of Lane and Daniel were all too clear.

After speaking with these 2 new gentlemen, I was pleasantly surprised.

They started off asking what I wanted from **my** fitness goals.

I let them know I wanted more energy, wanted to be lean and didn't want my whole life revolving in the kitchen.

I asked if I could eat the same thing every day.

Chicken and Potatoes.

They both said yes.

Plus, they gave some additional tips to make the journey more seamless.

Rather than trying to convert me to their tribe, they were more focused on providing value through their knowledge.

These 2 coached a lot of people like me.

Entrepreneurs who want to stay in shape, but aren't trying to compete for a body building show.

Therefore, I could tell they knew their market by the way they gave feedback.

Both of these individuals didn't try selling me anything.

Although I would not have remotely minded if they did.

Instead, they sent me blog articles they wrote to give more info and supplements which would help.

Then they said, *'if you have any more questions, don't hesitate to ask.'*

This is how our social bond formed.

Anytime they need something from me, I'm willing to hook them up as well.

The **Science of Getting Rich** is a tiny little book that can be read in a day.

The author, Wallace Wattles, brings up the concept of Use value and Cash Value.

Use value is anything that can be useful.

Me trying to sell a steak to a vegan is not smart.

It's because the vegan does not have USE for it.

Sure, I can do a lot of sales tactics to make the vegan momentarily have a lapse in judgment to get the sale.

However, that's not ethical.

Wallace says Use value MUST be provided before receiving Cash value.

Cash value is the money.

With this little formula, business can now be a vehicle for self improvement...

A way to build integrity and become a solid member of society.

Don't let mainstream entertainment fool you.

The rich are not evil.

A ton of the rich got rich by giving use value before taking cash value.

Did some do the opposite?

Did some take the cash through manipulative tactics while skimping on the use value?

Sure.

Corrupt people exist.

Just like a complex code will have bugs, a complex society will have people with poor character.

But to paint all business with that mindset is short sighted.

Deep inside, I couldn't take the money from the wealthy man because I knew I couldn't give him top tier use value on how to resolve his marriage with this wife.

That's a lane for someone else.

When I told him to seek someone else, he knew that I was a guy who would give Use before Cash.

That's the motto for the ArmaniTalks brand.

Long term thinking or no term thinking, playa.

So you may want to ask yourself:

'Am I abiding by this simple formula? Do I give more use before I ask for cash?'

This is also a brilliant formula for social skills as well.

The ability to make someone else feel important before you try making yourself feel important.

Business done right is social skills.

Yes, you heard it here folks.

So be a stand up person.

It'll all pay dividends in the grand scheme of things.

MISCOMMUNICATION

Last year, after the Covid cases, a lot of the gyms around my area got shut down.

So the people from the gyms ended up creating a home gym or skimping out on their workouts.

The gym I went to was called YouFit.

With that being shut down, I stayed active by buying a pullup bar, doing pushups and playing basketball.

As more time went by, there was a small gym in my neighborhood that opened up.

It's one of those tiny gyms with very minimal weights and a treadmill.

This should do for now...

As more time went by, I came to realize that the major gyms were opening up.

That means YouFit should be opening up as well.

I check the old location that I went to...

It's only 8 minutes away from where I live.

When I search for it, it's nowhere to be found.

Hm...that's strange.

So I look to see where the closest YouFit was.

And I see the closest one is 28 minutes away!

That may not seem like much.

But driving there and back, plus the occasional traffic makes it a 1 hour commute.
Multiple times a week.

I tried it out for a few days a couple of months back.
However, didn't like the drive.

The area in Tampa I live in is a bit strange with gyms.
It's either very cheap or very expensive.
I decided to go back to the local neighborhood gym.

Months pass...

This morning, I decide that I'm going to go back to YouFit.
Whatever, I'll suck it up and make the drive.

As I enter, there is a small woman with blonde hair and a mask on who greets me.

I told her I lost my gym card and if I could get a new one.
She asks me for my name and phone number.
I give it to her.

After looking into her system for some time, she looks at me and says, 'Sir, you're not a member.'

I look back at her confused.
I respond back with, *yes I am.*

Trust me.. I know.
Those monthly 13.99$ deductions in my bank account didn't go unnoticed lol.

Once again, she says I'm not a member.

I look back at her even more confused.
It writes "general manager" on her tag.
So she isn't some newbie hire.

We talk for a few and I say that I'll create a membership.
I guess I'll get the bill payment thing sorted out when I get back to my place.

I ask her for the basic plan.
She says, '10 dollars a month.'

As I'm about to give her my credit card, I decide to ask her a few more questions.
I ask her if she's **positive** that I'm not a member.

She says, 'yes.'

I then ask her a different styled question because it seems like she committed to me not being a member.
I told her I USED to be a member.
Does her system have information on past clientele?

That's when she looked at me and said,
'Well, Crunch gyms bought out a bunch of the other YouFit's. So if you're not a part of the YouFit that Crunch bought out, I can pull up your data.'

Something clicked....

I told her I'd be back.
Then I went into my car and looked up the nearest location of a Crunch gym.
It was 4 minutes away.

Once I get inside Crunch, a Spanish lady greets me.

I tell her that I used to be a member of YouFit and I think Crunch bought out the gym that I was a part of. Asked her to check if I was a member.

She checked and said,

'Yes, Arman Chowdhury. You are a member. Enjoy your workout!'

Click!

This was a learning moment in regards to communication.

I'm surprised the first YouFit lady never considered to say, *'Hey your gym may have been bought out by Crunch. You should double check with them before creating a membership with us.'*

Not even blaming her though.

It's because of a thing called **miscommunication**.

That's when people are approaching similar information from different perception maps.

I've bought up what a perception map is in my past emails.

So I'm not going to get too detailed.

Here's a quick summary.

This map is an accumulation of our desires, experiences, knowledge, cognitive complexity (rate of processing information) all jumbled into 1.

It's the sunglasses that we view reality from.

Everyone's perception map is different.

'Even identical twins who were near each other their entire lives?"

Yes, even the identical twins.

A TINY experience immediately makes a person's perception map **entirely** different than someone else's.

The YouFit lady simply could not process how I was saying that I was a member.

She heard the words.

But she did not have the experience of the 13.99$ being deducted every month from her bank account.

Had she seen the money deducted from her perception map, then I'm almost certain the Crunch insight would have CLICKED sooner for her.

When you can imagine that others are wearing a different sunglass of reality, miscommunications can still happen.

However, you reduce your likelihood of being misinterpreted to a high degree.

Even if the miscommunication does happen, it's easier to recalibrate from your end and not take things personally.

This allows the world view to open up.

Have you ever wondered why 2 people see the same things but report different experiences?

It's because they had micro to macro experiences which were vastly different from one another.

Empathy in a nutshell is being able to read someone's perception map without allowing your own biases to influence it.

So the next time a miscommunication is happening, fall back real quick.

HURT FEELINGS

I'm a tad bit strange at times.
We all are.

For me, pain fuels.
Makes it easier for me to write and think of better ideas.

I was talking to this big account a while back who was surprised I never blocked an account on Twitter.

Not that I say too many controversial things.
I try to have a balanced outlook of life.
I do my best to create a synergy between emotions and logic.

However, I have gotten a hand full, or *2 handfuls* of people who hated on me.
They tried to tempt me to block them.

Yet, I just didn't.
No strategy as to why back then.
Just didn't feel like it.

Nowadays, I came to realize that feelings serve as electricity for the body.
And shutting myself off from those feelings (good or bad) is not good in terms of creativity.

Storytelling comes down to experiencing the **full range** of the human spectrum.
Identify with the full coin rather than just one side.

It was the inner voice which said, *'don't block anyone. Screenshot mean comments. Use it as fuel.'*

What a ridiculous concept, I thought.
Yet, how practical it is.

I hate the concept of 'dealing' with things.
Although I've used the phrase a bunch of times in the spoken and written word before.

To deal with something creates a passive narrative.

Who do you think will recover faster?

-Jimmy, who is dealing with a breakup.
OR
-Mikey, who is thriving during a breakup.

I've gotten over a dozen of young men in their early 20s who had just gone through a breakup and they asked me how they were going to deal with it.

I'm not a relationship coach.
But what I can say is to change 'deal' to 'thrive.'
This narrative turns hurt feelings into fire feelings.

Set yourself on fire in order to come out stronger.
No matter what it is.

Kill your past self to be born again.
Killing in terms of limiting beliefs, narratives and even the micro sensations of your body.

The death of your old self only happens with **full** acceptance, not partial.

That's a lesson learned the hard way.

Emotions don't follow the same rules as logic.

In logic, when you try to subtract something, it happens.

When I take 1 away from 3, I know I'll get 2.

With emotions, subtracting can lead to multiplication.

I can try to subtract the feeling of sadness.

However, the feeling of sadness goes to the gym, uses hypertrophy, multiples in size and makes me more sad.

Therefore, I must accept.

Hurt has 4 letters.

Keyword is 'letters.'

Letters are not reality.

I don't block because I **need** the entire spectrum to be creative.

The good, the bad and the ugly.

All serves as fuel.

I suggest you do the same.

To kill your subpar self, accept your subpar self.

That's the surefire way to greatness.

A STORY ABOUT NOTHING

I went to a Korean BBQ spot a few weeks ago.
It was for a friend's birthday.

By the time I arrived, I was about to break a very long fast.
So I was hungry to say the least.

It was one of those fancy places.
Where the menu's were expensive.

I'm wary of places like this.
I have no problem paying a lot of money for food.
However, there's a catch.
I better get my money's worth.

I rather leave painfully full from a restaurant than moderately hungry.

After I order my food, I see that I have to cook the dish myself.
This place has some cool BBQ grills to heat the meat up in.
I start participating.

Once the food is done, I mix the meat with the sticky rice and begin eating.

And once I'm done.....
I felt like I didn't get my money's worth.

I'm staring at a 65 dollar bill while hearing my stomach growl.

I hear others near me saying, *'Oh my God, I'm just addicted to this place. It's my 3rd time here this week! I need to relax.'*

3rd time?

I couldn't fathom going back to that place unless it was for a special occasion.

A vice is defined as a wicked behavior, on Google.

I think that definition is too harsh.

I like to view a vice as a *quirk*.

Plenty of vices are prevalent among us.

I viewed those people who spend a lot on money on tiny portions of food as having a vice.

I would much rather go to Taco Bell and get a 5 dollar box.

Those people who I am considered having a vice for their fancy taste probably view ME as having the vice.

Taco Bell, really???

I believe vices are a reminder to make humans aware that they are people.

It helps them see that there are quirks among us and people can have completely different viewpoints.

I knew a kid who was obsessed with Oreos'.

Overall, seemed like a normal guy.

Had a side business, worked a job, had a family etc.

However, he would eat one box of Oreo's a day for a while..

That seems odd..

But if you look close enough, you may have a weird act like that too.

It's not about announcing it to others to let them know that you are one of them.

Instead, it's about using the vice to see how you can understand others.

I could not fathom how a lady went to that Korean BBQ place 3 times in 1 week.

That's because I'm evaluating value from my lens.

Value from my lens is food FILLING someone up.

However, value from her lens may have been the joy she got from using the cooking grill.

Anyways, this story was about nothing.

Yet, a lesson presented itself.

We judge other people's vices from a logical lens.

And we view our vices from a justification lens.

Flipping it creates massive change.

Justify other's vices temporarily to empathize.

Use logic to break down your own vices to self improve.

MAN'S BEST FRIEND

A couple of years ago, I went to Las Vegas for a marketing conference.

I was broke, so I barely had money for the plane ride.

Luckily, I knew someone else who was going to the same event.

His name was Jake.

Jake and I met in a forum for affiliate marketing. We eventually decided to create a little mastermind group to hold each other accountable.

5 total members in that group.

When Jake said he was going to the same conference, we decided to split an airbnb.

He said he'd book it.

Once he booked it, he gave me the amount that I owed him.

'Yo dude, just pay over 17.50$ for your half when you get the chance.'

17.50$??

We are staying in Vegas for 4 nights. How the heck did it come out so cheap?

When I asked him if he sent me the full amount, he said, *'yea man, I'm just as surprised.'*

I was a little suspicious.

Did this man book us in some bad neighborhood? No way can an Airbnb be that cheap.

We land in Vegas at night.

By the time we get to the location, it's 3 am.

The place we are staying at is huge!

Hm...guess Jake just ended up finding an amazing deal.

As we put in the code to get into the door, I notice the lights in the living room are on.

Once we enter, I see this elderly woman reading a newspaper.

She looks up at us and is like, *'Oh my! Such handsome men! I have been waiting for you. What took you guys so long?'*

Jake and I were surprised that she was up.

Heck, we were surprised that she was even there in the first place!

I guess he booked one of those spots where the owner stays with you.

She proceeded to give us a tour. Then she gave us a heavy meal which included turkey, mashed potatoes and macaroni and cheese.

Felt like this was Thanksgiving or something.

As I was eating, I noticed this Big black dog licking my feet.

He startled me at first because I didn't see the dog when initially coming in.

The more he licked on my feet, the more I snuck some food to him.

We eventually asked the woman what she did to have such a big mansion.

She let us know that her husband was a wealthy entrepreneur. He had just passed away recently.

Then she said,

'the Airbnb guests and the dog are the only things keeping me sane. My husband and I never had kids, so the last bit of my family is gone. My husband loved the dog. Would only cry when the dog was not feeling well. The dog cried when my husband died. I never got why my husband loved the dog so much. He was a brutish man. Now with my husband gone, I get why...'

It's like this lady has been waiting to speak to someone for the longest time.

Jake and I just listened without interrupting.

Nowadays, when I think about it, I wonder why that man cried only around his dog?

It's a pattern I've noticed for some time.

This is when strong people break down when their pet dies.

A few years back, my brother had a friend named Emily. And one day, her dog was extremely sick.

Since I was the only one with a car, I took my bro, Emily and this sick dog to the vet.

As I was in the vet, I observed the different people's body language. It looked somber and depressing.

Eventually, a vet took Emily and her dog to the back. I was told to stay in the waiting room.

While I was waiting, I recall seeing this big grizzly looking man coming out of the back area with his teenage daughter.

The girl looked rather stoic. But this large man was crying uncontrollably.

It got to a point where he slugged his way to the payment area and had his elbows on the desk with his head down.

The daughter rubbed her dad's back to imply, *'it'll all be okay.'*

Not to sound sexist...
But I thought it would be the other way around.

I thought the daughter would be crying and the dad would be consoling her.
No...
It was the other way around.

I have no clue who this man was. However, to me, he looked strong. Yet, due to his dog passing, he was momentarily weak.
He was gripping his former dog's leash....

Why do strong people break apart when their pet dies?
This is an interesting time to learn about psychology.

I have no facts, but here is my theory.
It's because a pet never judges.

Whether someone wants to hear this or not, people judge all the time. In an ideal world, we never judge a book by its cover.
However, the subconscious mind does not care.

Judging can happen in a matter of microseconds.

With this judgment taking place, personalities are filtered. This is why the 'just be authentic' phrase is very vague.
We act differently with different people.

After a certain period, I think humans accept reality for what it is.
They become cognizant of this 'judging' process.

-Some break apart. They can't believe they are being judged.

-Others try to fit in. In order to try to stop the judging from taking place, they modify their personality.

-A few move forward regardless. They work on a bigger vision which outweighs their tendency to care about the judgment.

With strong people, they look at humans one way and their pets another way.

Their pets see their authentic self.
With the pet, the strong person does not have to deliver any tangibles.

The pet only wants the owner's attention.
Plus food.

Food is common sense.
But the attention is what's key.

Just like the adult eventually became aware that humans judge…
The adult also became aware that the pet doesn't judge.

When the second realization is made, rapport is strengthened.
And a human to animal communication morphs into a lifelong friend to lifelong friend communication.

Few people accept others through the ups and downs.
But the pet is one of those creatures which can look at a human beyond duality.

Anyways, that's my personal theory.

Strong people are allowed to be weak around their pet without being judged for it.

Which is why they break apart when man's best friend dies.

I break down the whole psychology regarding all this because this newsletter gives a 4D perspective regarding human nature and psychology.

If you want to understand the movie, then you gotta understand how the movie was created.

That requires understanding the movie directors, script writers, technical team and much more.... rather than only watching what's on the screen...

MEN AND WOMEN

I wrote a tweet a few days ago which ended up picking up traction.

Today, I'm going to break down that tweet.

I wrote:

-*Women view maturity as the ability to express emotions*

-*Men view maturity as the ability to control emotions*

General heuristics

I threw in the last line because there is always someone who is like, 'not all men' or 'not all women.'

Agreed.

However, this was a general pattern.

Men and women picked up this tweet and shared it.

For the most part, I didn't see any one saying that I was flat out wrong.

This shows how certain words are up for interpretation.

Maturity being one of them.

For the rest of the email, I'm going to be speaking in general terms, so if that bugs you, oh well buddy.

Women view maturity as the ability to express emotions.

Emotions are a flux of energy plus a perception attached to it.

There was a time I saw a viral tweet where a women tweeted :

'I hate it when I'm sharing a problem with my husband... And he just starts solving it. Like geez, can you just let me vent?'

People were putting laughing emojis in the tweet.

I saw it as a class on psychology.

The man immediately went into problem solving mode because his logical mind fired up.

However, the woman was sharing the problem not to have it solved.

But rather, to vent.

Women share problems with those who they trust.

So when a woman is opening up in a conversation setting and going deeper, especially with the opposite gender, it means trust is being built.

They feel safe in the man's presence.

For men, they love to solve problems for people they care for. It's almost instinct.

So in this situation, when the husband hears that his wife is bringing up a problem, it is 2nd nature for him to want to make it go away.

Different languages....

For men, expressing emotions can be a bonus.

However, when men measure other men, the first thing that comes to their mind is how well can they control their emotions.

Winners build.

Bitchy men destruct.

I've seen guys like that.

Makes snarky comments on the sidelines, gossips excessively and takes more value than they give.

I rather lose in the battlefield rather than win on the sidelines.

Top tier men find the ability to control emotions to be a valuable trait.

Because top tier men build.

In the building process, a roller coaster of emotions are experienced.

From joy, to anger, to depression, to joy once again.

This man should be able to deal with these emotions.

For the ArmaniTalks brand, I've dropped the phrase 'EQ' many times.

Emotional Quotient.

Emotional Intelligence.

I have a hybrid definition.

I believe men and women should aim to strive to express emotions **and** control emotions.

By express, I don't mean just sit down and talk about feelings all day.

I mean to know that others are not mind readers.

You should be able to express yourself rather than intentionally doing jerky body language movements....hoping someone can tell something is wrong.

In terms of controlling emotions, I don't mean suppression.

I mean the ability to do alchemy.

Turn anger into creative fuel.

Turn sadness into a chance to introspect.

Since most of my readers are men, let me show what this looks like in practice real quick.

I knew this one guy a couple of years back who did website development.

A Russian guy.

This guy was gifted.

But didn't know **how to negotiate** at all.

His clients took advantage of him & paid him scraps.

On the phone, this Russian would be all smiley and friendly.

But after he hung up, he'd vent that he was annoyed by the blatant disrespect.

I don't think the customers were blatantly being disrespectful.

I believe the customers were just behaving how customers normally behave.

The Russian should have expressed his emotions in a way where he stands up for himself and doesn't create an enemy in the process.

No one was going to read his mind.

This was a situation where a man should be able to express his emotions.

Business at the end of the day is people skills with money involved.

So if you can't stand up for yourself, don't expect others to.

Controlling emotions is king.

That's modern alchemy.

The ability to express eloquently is queen.

That's an amplifier.

Do both and you skyrocket your maturity and build thick skin in the process.

CONTRADICTIONS

There are tons of different writing styles out there.

Some prefer long essays.

Others prefer short stories.

And some prefer poetry.

I have always preferred short stories.

To get more specific, I have a writing style that I like to call, *artistic engineering*.

2 very contradictory phrases.

The artist side of me likes to keep it simple and sometimes I use colloquial language (informal) because it speaks more to the spirit.

The engineer side of me likes to keep it logical. I like my writing to be grounded in reality & not fantasy.

I came to realize that this writing style can be very contradictory.

As a matter of fact, I think this style will only resonate with a small group of people.

Which was always my intention.

I rather have 10 people who get my style vs, 1000 mass audience people who just don't get it.

Recently, I put my new book, **Word Play**, on the Amazon Kindle Unlimited program.

Long story short, its sort of like Netflix for book readers.

And the author gets paid for each page read.

I came to see that new people had discovered the ArmaniTalks brand.

In the beginning of the book, I give a free short story course for the people who bought the book.

A few people claimed the free offer.

Which led them to my website.

From my website, they discovered my YouTube, blog, and some discovered this email list.

I got an email recently from a new reader saying that my writing style was unique to him.

He couldn't tell if I was a poet or an essayist.

For a while, Word Play was the #1 New Release on Poetry Anthologies.

So, many people who read it probably thought they were about to read a poetry book.

I like it when someone can't tell what kind of a writer I am.

A famous filmmaker said that too much logic saps away creativity.

I like to keep people guessing.

When I got the question if I'm a poet or an essayist, I said in a humorous tone, both.

The answer is, it really depends.

Discovering my writing style is an ongoing process.

One that will go on for life.

So you can say I am creating the style rather than discovering it.

CAN'T STOP, WON'T STOP

Get paid to practice.
Just kidding.

Or am I?

Imagine you want to make a career out of being a teacher.
This is something that you put a lot of thought behind.

One day, you see one of your friends struggling with a subject.
Let's say it's calculus 3.

It just so happens that you are brilliant in that subject.
You could solve problems with your eyes closed.

Your friend asks you to tutor him.
But you don't feel like it.

That's when he says that he'll pay you 20 dollars for 1 hour.
Hm...20 dollars?
Okay fine, you'll teach him.

Within 20 minutes, he begins asking questions away.
At this point, you are being tested on whether you know the topic
or not.

Each question he asks, each question you answer.
You're practicing the art of teaching.
And you're getting paid for it.

The money may not be high.

However, it's the concept that matters.

You are getting monetary value regarding something that you *want* to do.

There are different subjects I believe a person should be curious about at one point or another.
One of those topics is neuroplasticity.

The more I learn about this topic, the more eager I am to practice something.
I view it as coding humans.

In a nutshell, one of the laws, Hebb's law, implies that neurons that fire together, wire together.

This is good news because the neurons in our brain are chatty.
They like to talk to each other a lot.

When we practice a certain act, the neurons starts talking in a certain way with one another.
That 'certain way' determines the proficiency of a task.

The more they chat through repetition and mindful practice, the more cables start to be formed among them.
The neural cables turn a mindful act into a mindless one.
So too much cognitive effort is not always required.

At this point, a lot of people are aware of the neuroplasticity subject.

What I came to notice is that when you bring up this topic with a certain group of people, they immediately blurt out:
'I already know about the topic.'
Before even letting you finish.

After they recite what they know about the topic, they go back to normal.

It's like a part of them wanted to show how smart they are.

I look at these people.

Pudgy.

Bad habits.

Impulsive.

You know this knowledge of changing your internal state by controlling your nervous system.

But what have you done with it?

Fat boi.

Nothing.

All the knowledge without application means nothing.

That's why I write a newsletter everyday.

It's been over a 1000+ days and I haven't missed a beat.

I don't do this because I am bored.

I'm doing this to practice writing.

Nothing ever comes easy to me.

It's just a matter of showing up, over and over.

Nowadays, what I've noticed is something a tad bit spooky.

'What?'

Sometimes, the newsletters write themselves.

'Yea right!'

No, I'm serious.

It's not that strange of a concept.

You know how you sometimes get behind the wheel...
And you're already at your destination?
That's the car driving itself.
Mainly because you put the reps in.

That's what happens with the newsletters at times.
I believe one of my most impactful email's was, Fire in the Belly.

I wrote it over a year ago.

That was the email that lit a fire in some people's minds.
Got a few emails back saying, 'yo man, this one really woke me up. Thanks.'

Well, that was one of the emails that wrote itself!

I wrote a tweet awhile back saying that you should practice so much that you begin surprising yourself.
I didn't mean this in an ambiguous sense.

I meant this in a very practical and spiritual sense.

-Practical, because you have measurable outputs from your practice session.
-Spiritual, because you begin thinking big and wondering if you've been holding back on your potential.

Practice is one thing.
But knowledge behind practice is a whole different ball game.

DRUGS

I don't know if it's just me...

But the 8 hour a night sleeping routine hasn't been working for me.

Whenever I sleep 7-9 hours in a night, I end up feeling groggy the next day.

For me, 5-6 hours works very well.

I feel energized then.

No coffee needed.

I'm no sleep expert.

But I heard that not getting 7-9 hours of sleep is very bad.

Then again, how are these studies measured?

Do I need to get all 7-9 hours at once?

Or can I sleep 5-6 hours and get a couple of power naps in throughout the day?

As I was pondering on this question of sleep, I had a memory recall of this guy named Shah Rukh Khan.

If you've never heard of him, he's one of the most famous actors in Bollywood.

I believe he is one of the highest paid entertainers in the world.

What has been captivating about his career is his consistency after so many years.

I remember watching his movies when I was a little kid.

Nowadays, he is still making movies!

A couple of years back, he was having this interview with Jeff Bezos.

One of the questions he asked Jeff was, *'What do you think is a waste of time that others deem important?'*

You could tell the question sort of puzzled Jeff.

So, Shah Rukh Khan offered his version of the answer.

He said, *'I think sleep is a waste of time. I hate sleeping.'*

Jeff was trying to be polite.

But you could tell by his body language that the answer caught him off guard.

Doesn't this man know how much sleep is needed for a human to perform at peak levels??

I wonder what makes consistent people consistent.

How has Shah Rukh Khan remained the king of Bollywood for so long?

You may find the answer peculiar like his sleep answer.

But here it goes.

He views his work as a drug.

He has mentioned plenty of times that he feels a sudden rush when he is acting.

Something about creating a new character out of thin air makes him feel alive. Plus, he loves the creative process of making a movie.

Most of my readers are from the US. So, I'm sure you're familiar with Hollywood. You may have thought that I was making a typo earlier when I said Bollywood .

Nope. Bollywood is the filmmaking industry of India.
There movies are very different.
Tons of songs, and dancing mixed into the plot.

When I see a movie like that, I'm thinking...*damn, these actors in Bollywood need to be versatile.*
They need to be in shape, know some dance moves, be able to lip sync, and act!

Shah Rukh Khan has been effortlessly consistent because he has viewed his work as a drug.

Everyone has vices and demons.
No need to admit them to others
But at least admit them to yourself.

I had a friend who was able to stop smoking cigarettes by replacing it with comic books.
He nowadays runs an animation channel on YouTube.

A drug is typically associated with negativity.
I believe it's time to associate drugs with positivity.
The good kind, of course.

Find something that makes you feel **alive** like Shah Rukh Khan comes alive when acting.

My advice is to write. I think that's one of the healthiest drugs out there.
Write by hand first so you win your body over.

Check out my new creative writing journal, *Idea Machine*.

333 creative writing prompts ranging from fantasy, to self development, philosophy and much more.

You will be given a random prompt daily where you can flex your creative muscles.

The benefits of writing in the Idea Machine are:

-clearer thinking
-better content topics for your business
-improved conversation skills
-sharper writing skills to persuade others

And most importantly..
A drug that adds to your life, rather than takes from it.

LEARNING TO READ

A small fragment of the population read for fun.
The rest view it as work.

I'm not against video games, watching tv, and other leisure activities.
To each their own.

But I do want to give you some tips on learning HOW to read.
And by **how**, I'm referring to making reading fun.

First things first, the question is....
Why are you reading?

Is there an underlying narrative?
This is where I think a lot of people mess up.

I believe you should have a side hustle.
Because it gives your reading journey a target.

I'm sure you heard the quote that the average CEO reads 50+ books a year.
They are reading like that because they are working on building an organism.
That organism just happens to be a business.

Without working on any organism, whether it be a business, your body (fitness), another person (like raising a kid), reading will always feel like work.

When you are working on improving SOME kind of organism, that's when the game changes.

Now reading is like solving a big puzzle.

For the 2nd step, I'd say to ask for less book recommendations.

'Why shouldn't I ask for too much reading recommendations in the beginning?'
Because spotting the wrong book is just as important as spotting the right book.

You see, the viewpoint of content is subjective.
'What would you say determines what I find valuable?'
Your experiences.

A person who is working on building a business will gravitate more towards a business book.
A person who is trying to be a sci-fi author will gravitate more towards a sci-fi book.

By spotting which books do NOT resonate with you, you'll be able to better spot when you stumbled on the right one.

3rd step is to have somewhat of a discipline.
For myself, I try to read 20 minutes a day.

I don't say 2 hours a day.
Because I don't know if I can commit that many hours based on my schedule.
For others, they may be able to.

That's up to you.
But by saying, 'Yo, read 20 minutes,' I am capable of meeting my bare minimum requirements.

Here's one bonus tip.

This may not work for you.

But it works for me:

Rotate between a nonfiction and fiction book during your reading session.

Because certain times, you may be reading a book, then after some time, you start getting bored.

That's when you can put that book down and open the other one.

By having 2 books in your rotation, it feels like you are entering more worlds.

This bonus tip may fall flat for some.

So don't try it for too long if it has you feeling distracted.

I do want to stress though....

If you're naturally not the type of person who enjoys reading for fun...

Then I recommend starting to work on some sort of organism.

Have a network that needs constant maintenance.

And target your reading efforts around that!

That's what begins the readers journey.

If you want to take it a level further to commit to the reader's journey, buy a bookshelf.

These are all suggestions.

Ultimately, you want to decide which path works best for you.

DO IT YOURSELF

The concept of DIY has always been popular.
This is a way to empower someone when you think about it.

DIY = Do It Yourself.

One type of videos I enjoy watching are when engineers build stunning inventions with household items.
Sometimes, they will buy the parts & make inventions out of nowhere.

This doesn't only apply to engineering.
It can apply to other fields as well.

Let's say a woman has been watching a cooking show for a while.
She practiced the dishes that she learned on TV.
Now she wants to create her **own** recipe.

After a string of failures, she finally creates something that tastes amazing.
Do it yourself.

I made a very staggering realization recently.
'What was that?'

Nowadays, people are having a DIY approach to their personality.

I came to find out a lot of the topics I cover in my YouTube channel also resonates with singers.
A few people who discovered my channel were recommended my videos when they were looking for singing solutions.

Problems singers face include:
-*Cracks in the voice.*
-*Running out of breath.*
-*Rapid heartbeat, etc.*

When they searched for solutions, somehow they stumbled onto my channel.

That was never my intention.
However, they used my speaking videos for a **personal problem** regarding singing.

I came to realize content serves as Lego pieces.
It's up to the person who is consuming the content to decide what kind of building they want to make.

In this case, the building is personality.

Nowadays, we live in an era where personality is more like a buffet.
But due to outdated paradigms, the masses think dinner is still being served.

They sit their waiting for their routine plates.
Getting agitated that the waiter didn't ask them what they want to eat.
They are unaware to the fact that they are the ones who get up and fix their own plates.

You can alter your personality at will.
The trick is deciding what type of personality you want.

I believe this is the future of content creation.
Rather than niching down too much...

Create themes.

Niching down works.
However, I've noticed that sometimes it becomes difficult to talk about the same topic too much.
Eventually, it builds a distaste.

Rather than beating a dead horse, have a theme.
This is a general gist.

So rather than a YouTube creator talking only about growth strategies for YouTube.
They can talk about the theme of content creation in general.
And YouTube just happens to fall under their umbrella.

Now someone can use your content with a DIY mindset.

Not everyone is trying to be a creator.
That's all good.

The main takeaway is knowing that you can change your personality.
It's something that others do not consider.
'They never consider it?'
Probably sometimes. But it's wishful thinking for them.

The personality is not like height.
The height cannot change after some time.
Your personality most likely can.

'Why did you say most likely?'
Because it takes a while to notice the changes.
Only a miniscule amount will wait it out & execute till those changes become apparent...

FIRST IMPRESSIONS

There are a few people who I remember meeting for the first time.

But for the most part, I wonder, 'how did I meet them again?'

First impressions mean more when you don't plan on having an opportunity again.

I think first impressions are important..

But putting all your eggs in that basket creates a scarcity mindset.

You start moving like a clown.

I had this public speaking coach 2 years ago.

Great guy.

There was an exercise he made me do that I didn't like.

It happened when I made him aware that I had a decent sized following on Twitter.

He was baffled when I told him it was over 10,000 people.

He was in his 60s.

So numbers like that weren't that common when he did business.

In the initial stages, he wanted to know what this "twitter thing" could do.

I explained what it was.

Then I told him about the periscope feature.

Back then, you could do live videos on twitter.

Even answer questions in real time.

When he heard that feature, he was like, 'Let's have you do some more of those videos!'

Which I did.

I post them on YouTube every now and then.
Those are the ones which are extremely grainy for some reason.

I noticed the advice he kept giving me was how to open the video.
He would place *a lot* of focus on the opener. Didn't talk much about the middle or close.

'We HAVE to get their attention in the beginning.'
Otherwise, they will tune out.

That seemed like a reasonable thing for a coach to say.
However, something about the concept just felt off.
Didn't feel natural.

Well, recently, I've been reading this book called the **Long Tail by Chris Anderson**.
Highly recommend checking out this book if you are a creative person who is looking to get into business.

Long story short, he talks about these things called the long tail in searches.
The parts which seem unnoticeable, but they aren't.

Let me give you an example.

When you picture music, I'm sure you think 'what are the hits' first.
Same with music companies.
They want the hits.

So in the front of the tail, it's a huge spike.

All representing the most popular songs.

The more you go down, the more you notice the spike starts to dwindle in size.

That's when the long tail starts to take over.

The long tail includes the songs that don't often go noticed.

But what was **stunning** was that the tail NEVER goes to 0.

Which means, there is someone always downloading some of the most obscure songs out there.

'The Hillbillies go to Pickle Town' song.

Never heard of it?

Well, that song gets 3 downloads a month.

(I made up the name of that song by the way.)

What Chris Anderson started to wonder was....'How much revenue do these tiny songs bring in for the entire company?'

After running the numbers, he noticed in some companies, the long tails bring in more revenue than the actual hits!!

Just imagine.

10,00,0000 *The Hillbillies go to Pickle Town* songs and one Britney Spears *Oops I Did it Again* song.

10,000,000 long tails vs a hit.

Long tail has a shot to bring in more revenue.

'Armani....You were supposed to be talking about first impressions. Why are you talking about business?'

Because I'm about to make a stunning parallel.

I came to realize the concept of the long tail happens with social skills and digital content as well!

YouTube has a feature where you can see how long people watch your videos.

Typically, a 35% watch rate is pretty good.

For the old school periscope videos I did, they are so grainy when I try uploading them on YouTube.

Plus, the audio lags.

I'll be saying something and the audio catches up 10 seconds later.

No way can someone finish these garbage periscope videos all the way through, right?

WRONG!!!

There's a spike in the beginning when people are first clicking on the video.

It dwindles.

Just like with music companies who have hits and it starts to go to regular songs.

But as the video progresses, I notice the long tail NEVER gets to 0..

Some people are always watching the video all the way through.

Even with my daily newsletter, I can't quite validate the number, but I'm sure the long tail readers read all the way through.

That's when I started putting together WHY my old school public speaking coach's exercise did not resonate with me.

It's because my future self was telling me to talk to the long tall.

I didn't want to talk to someone who opens the video and needs me to coax them to keep watching.

That's where this whole talk ties into first impressions.

I think relying on first impressions too much conditions the hit mentality.

It's like we have to put on this big show when we are meeting someone.

First impressions can matter.

But what matters more is the long game.

How much are you showing up over a long period of time?

If a person was that turned off by a first impression you made, then:

-That's probably because you really fucked up. Take accountability

Or

-Because the person was just an iffy kind of person. They were never going to rock for you like that.

I noticed that targeting the long tail gives a more poised look on life.

The tail never goes to 0.

-Some people will rock for you no matter what.

-Some people will never rock for you no matter what.

Question is, which group are you going to focus most of your attention on?

MULTIPLE LESSONS

I just wrapped up a 2.5 hour podcast with LifeMathMoney today.

During the conversation, something happened that got me thinking about learning, knowledge and laziness.

Recently, I released my book **Word Play** on Amazon.

During the conversation, I bought up the book.

Told LifeMathMoney it was a book of short stories on a variety of topics dealing with soft skills.

He was intrigued and asked if I could share one of the stories.

I quickly shuffled through a bunch of stories in my mind and decided to tell him the one of the tuna man.

If you're a new reader, the tuna man story was about a rude man who would give the employees at Subway a hard time.

I was one of the employees.

I called him tuna man because he would always order a tuna sub.

I thought if I memorized his order that he would like me more.

Instead, when I showed I memorized his order, he got livid.

He yelled at me and told me to stop observing him.

Younger me got my feelings hurt and personalized it.

Until the next day, I saw him yelling at my 2 other coworkers.

Suddenly, the hurt turned into humor.

The ultimate lesson was that we personalize something when we think it's ONLY happening to us.

When we see it's happening to others as well, the tendency to personalize melts away.

LifeMathMoney was listening along.

After hearing my story, he got a different lesson from it.

The moral he got was that some people are just jerks.

You can do your best to impress them.

But it will never be enough.

So focus on those people who aren't the jerks.

The fact that LifeMathMoney got a different impression was great news for me.

That was my whole purpose of the book.

I believe communication skills is one of those subjects that you can't really learn through lectures.

"Do this, this, and this...and boom, now you know communication."

Some topics, you can give that lecture approach to.

However, for a lot of other topics, you want the lesson to be open to interpretation.

I used everyday occurrences and showed lessons can be sparked from that.

So when I shared the story, LifeMathMoney processed my experiences from his own experiences.

Leading to a different interpretation.

This is personally why I dislike 2 things:

-Art critics

-The saying, 'there is no such thing as a new idea.'

The first 1...
I don't listen to any art critics.
Nothing personal against them.
But I think they just get in the way.

I would rather listen to the audience rating over a critic's rating.
Still, I don't take the audience rating as seriously either.
Tons of people are sheep.
They think whatever the other person next to them thinks.

The less middlemen in between me and the art, the better.
I'll decide if I like the book.
Song.
Movie.

You stay out of my way buddy.

The second thing I dislike is the quote, 'there is no such thing as a new idea.'
I would say it depends.

Sure, the end product may be the same.
An example is with my tuna man story.
My insight was, 'we only personalize something when we think the act is only happening to us. We stop personalizing when we acknowledge it happens to others as well.'

Has someone from the vast sea of existence reached the same conclusion before?
Yea, I'm sure they have.

So what?

I doubt they reached that insight from the same experiences that I had in order to learn it.

In this case, I'm more concerted with the how rather than the what.

I think the quote 'there is no such as an new idea' gets people lazy.

All these people talk the same.

Then they will justify talking the same with:

 'didn't you hear? There's no such thing as a new idea.'

They say this with a big goofy smile on their face.

I'm a fan of unique content.

Something that is impossible to Google, because you have 0 clue how to phrase the Google query.

More people need to be thinking like that.

An idea is not this finite thing that cannot be stretched.

It's not like a table that is fixed.

That's what people who fall in love with that ridiculous quote think.

I've seen people use shaming language on others who thinks that quote is bullshit.

'Just imagine how arrogant you must be to think that you've discovered something new. You aren't that smart.'

No one is saying that.

What is being said is that the BUILD UP to the insight is where the magic happens.

The BUILD UP is what gets someone else's experiences involved.

That's what penetrates the subconscious mind.

That's what makes someone think,

'Wow, this is a person I have never met. But I see myself in him.'

That was the intention of Word Play.

Which is why I'm happy that LifeMathMoney got a different lesson from the story.

Our background shapes a large party of our reality.

That's what leads to *multiple lessons* from a single story.

SPOTLIGHT EFFECT

Last year, I went to a wedding where I didn't know many people.
Thought it was going to be awkward.

In the morning reception, I came to find out one of my fraternity brother's was going to be at the wedding.
I hadn't seen him in years.

As we are catching up, he said he stumbled across my ArmaniTalks website. He said he liked what I was doing.

He said he was glad to know a 'motivational speaker.'

If you've followed me for sometime, I've told this story before.
But today, I'm taking it from a different angle. If you're a new reader, then this story is new to you.

I respect the motivational speaking grind.
But I do not consider myself that.
I consider myself a storyteller.
I don't care if someone feels motivated or not after reading my stuff. The intention I move with is to give the truth. That's why I have a fire in my logo. Fire represents truth.

It is what it is.

I'm not over here trying to correct him and give him a lecture.
I let him say his comments & we go about catching up.

Later in the wedding, he introduces me to his girlfriend.
He's like, 'Hey Stacy, this is the motivational speaker I was telling you about!'

Here we go again.

I still don't want to correct him.
Especially in front of his girl.
I play along.

I'm thinking it's the end of it.
Not quite.

After some time, his girlfriend comes up and starts talking to me.
I already have a feeling what is going to happen.

Imagine you go to a party & your back is hurting.
You come to find out one of the people in the party is a chiropractor.

You have some decorum.
You're certain he's dealing with backs all day. That's the last thing he wants to talk about in this party.
Plus, you feel uncomfortable asking for free advice.

So you go this fellow.
Spark up causal conversation.
Then you're like, 'ouchhhh!!'
Touching your back & wincing in pain.

This fellow is like, 'what's wrong?'
You say, 'my back has been killing me!'

Now you're hoping for HIM to volunteer and be like, 'Let me take a look. I am a chiropractor!'

That's the vibe I got from this girl.

She tells me that she started a new job.
She's normally really confident.
However, in this job, she feels nervous.

Her voice gets soft, body language weakens & she seems disinterested.
She found out recently that her coworkers found her to be rude.

She's not rude, she's nervous.
I could tell she wanted me to motivate her out of this dilemma.

I decided I'd let her answer her own concerns.
Why did SHE think she was normally confident but at work, she was different?

Because I want to prove myself, she said.

-Don't you always want to prove yourself?

But it's different at work, she said.

-Why is it different at work?

I've been working my entire life for this job, she said.

-Does that mean you're putting more pressure on yourself?

Tons of pressure, she said.

-What happens when you normally put a lot of pressure on yourself?

I move different. I move stiff. I move awkward.....she said...

She was describing the Spotlight Effect.
When there is an **imaginary** spotlight over us, making us think that all our moves are being observed.

It's an illusion crafted by the ego.
Ego is node centered.

Node centered means that it's looking out for itself.
Imagine a home office setup.
A minimalist design.

Desk, chair, laptop, mouse, screen.
Imagine if the mouse thought all eyes were on it.
And it was feeling pressure.

You as the user would assure the mouse that it is a **part** of the system.
It isn't the full system.

The mouse feels more pressure to perform.
While it is you that will do the performing.
The mouse is simply a tool.

When the mouse realizes it's a tool, it can be calm.
When it's calm, it can function within the system.

As I talked to this girl, I came to realize that her lifelong dream to be in this job was causing her to think that *she* was the system.
Just like the mouse thought that it was the home office.

After we talked, she realized that she was accidentally being egotistical.

When we picture "egotistical", the first thing that can come to mind is someone who is smug.

That's not always the case.

Often, it can be someone who is fearful.

She was becoming egotistical because the narrative of finally having the job caused her to get attached.

And she didn't want to lose it.

-*The tighter she held, the brighter the spotlight got.*

-*The brighter the spotlight got, the stiffer she got.*

-*The stiffer she got, the ruder she was perceived by her coworkers.*

It's time to let go.

I came to find out that her coworkers had a strong distaste towards her.

That's what this girl made it seem like.

Which is a good thing.

'A good thing??'

Yea. One of the best times to overcome the Spotlight Effect is when you're down.

Just like one of the best times to overcome speech anxiety is right after you choked.

How much worse can it get?

Not anymore worse.

Might as well continue.

I just asked her questions.
Which gave her clarity.
That clarity ended up giving her motivation.

Spotlight Effect is when you are being the mouse who lost sight of the bigger picture.
Aim to **plug** into a system.
You are rarely the entire system.

A systems thinker looks at the big picture.
The bigger the picture, the more the light dims over time.

NAME DROPPING

Conversation's can often mask poor concentration skills.

It's because you have someone to bounce ideas off.

And it's tougher to spot how well you can speak without bouncing ideas off someone.

May seem like a left field thing of me to say.

Social skills can mask poor concentration skills?

At times, yes.

Try talking in front of a camera on ONE topic for 7-9 minutes.

This requires skills.

It can hurt the head.

The mind is like, 'whoa, what are you doing?'

Even when you talk to yourself in the car, you are probably not staying on 1 topic for long. You are hopping from topic to topic...

Being able to speak for a long time on your own is a special skillset.

This unlocks the potential of opportunities that the mind is capable of.

Just like solo **speaking requires skill**, another act that requires skill is building a brand without incessant namedropping.

Bringing up names every now and then is one thing.

However, when a brand is *centered* around talking about other people, I always keep them at arms length.

Sure, there are gossip channels who serve value to a segment of the market.

Not hating on the grind.

I still think there is a **special skillset** required in building a brand solely focused on ideas.

Last week, a popular channel called Fresh and Fit were getting attacked left and right.

Long story short, they started conflicting with a big channel named Aba and Preach.

Words were said.

Enemies were created.

Fresh and Fit lost over 30,000+ subscribers in a span of a few days.

Their recent videos were getting flooded with dislikes.

Their fans were turning on them.

Smaller channels smelled blood.

Here was Fresh and Fit, a colossal 400,000 subscriber account stumbling.

It was time for the smaller channels to rise.

The tiny channels would double down on the Fresh and Fit hate, provide commentary and their own thoughts on the brand.

Within a couple of days, tiny accounts began to balloon up.

One of the accounts started with 580 subscribers before the Fresh and Fit debacle and grew up to 13,500 subscribers during it.

It goes to show that name dropping others can be a lucrative strategy.

But is it a fulfilling one?

I don't know.

Fulfilling is a subjective phrase that means different things to different people.

What I do know is that riding the coattails of others proves a concept which has held true time and time again:

What comes fast goes fast.

In a few days to weeks, this Fresh and Fit debacle will be a thing of the past.

For the new channels who grew by name dropping others, the question is:

Now what?

There will be a group who capitalize on the new people.

They will talk about other people.

Give more feedback on cultural commentary.

And build a brand.

While another fragment of the smaller channels will drift off into the abyss.

They will learn the painful way that namedropping others is not a viable long term strategy.

Every now and them, names need to be dropped to make a point.

Sort of like what I'm doing in this email, by bringing up Fresh and Fit.

But when that's the only content material, a question to ask is:

*How many **tangible skills** are you building?*

-Are you **learning the art of thinking**?
-Creating ideas, testing & articulating?
-Or riding the coattails of other creators?

Negativity sells.
Don't listen to what people say.
Watch what people do.

Negativity will sell to the masses.
There will always be smaller accounts namedropping bigger accounts to rise up.

This isn't something that is happening recently.
If you study history, this behavior has always been common.

When it's all said and done, a minority (never the majority) will put in the work.
Will invest in their micro skills.

They will learn how to hold a conversation with others.
But they are never reliant on others.

Put them in a room by themselves, and they can still articulate a topic + stay on topic for however long you need them too.

This is a communication ninja.
Many hats.
1 identity.

This is the path of a winner.

THE TICKING TIME BOMB

Over a decade ago, I had a cousin from overseas visit and stay over for the summer with my family.

During his time staying with us, my brother & I bonded with this cousin.

We talked about our adventures, played games together & would watch tv till late at night.

I was getting my cousin into reality tv shows.

One particular show was, *I Love Money*.

This is when contestants from other popular shows would gather on an island and compete for a 250,000 dollar check.

This program was entertaining.

Late at night, my cousin would grab a bunch of donuts and watch with me and my brother.

One thing that my cousin would do a lot was punch my arm.

He'd do it in a way where for the first few times, I wouldn't feel the hits as much.

But since he kept hitting me in the same are, I'd start to feel pain.

He'd do it on autopilot.

Just randomly punching me on the arm while he was watching TV.

This annoyed me.

I told him to stop doing it.

He would stop.

Then, as a few days passed on by...
He'd begin doing it again!

There were 2 couches in the living room.
One long couch & one short couch.

My brother would lie on the long couch.
So he would occupy the whole thing.
My cousin and I would share the short couch together.

I was non-confrontational at the time.
So didn't want to aggressively be like, 'STOP hitting me!! Damn.'

Plus, he was warming up to me at this point.
I didn't want want hurt the interaction.

However, this was becoming bothersome.

One day, we are returning from a late night trip from Keywest.
A bunch of the family members are in a large van.
I'm sitting in the back with my cousin.

Rather than punching me this time, he puts his palm on my face & pushes it.
Not quite a slap.
But close to it.

That's when I had a knee jerk response & hit him back on the face.
And this wasn't close to a slap.
It was a real slap.

He looked back at me in the darkness and was like, 'What the fuck! Why did you slap me for? I was just joking.'

I didn't know why myself.
It's like my body did it for me.
And my mind was catching up...

I apologized to him.
Said I was half asleep.
He quickly forgave me.

Even though he forgave me, I think I slapped him like that because of all the times he kept punching me on autopilot.
The bruises on my left arm were starting to stack up.

At this point in my life, I was a Nice Guy.
I felt emotions like others.
However, didn't feel comfortable verbalizing it.
A lot of holding in.

One day, we had guests at the house.
My cousin was lying on his stomach watching TV.

The other guests are talking.
Some sitting on the floor.
And some lying down.

At this point, I was close to my cousin.
Decided to play a joke on him.

I was eating a Samosa.
Which is an pastry with ground beef inside it.

This Samosa was hot, but not too hot.
I put it on his back thinking it would startle him.

However, he didn't notice.
The Samosa just rested on his back.

The joke fell flat.
Once I pulled the Samosa off him....
I was startled!!!

There it was..
An oily triangle imprint on his amazing white Hugo Boss shirt.

This was my cousin's favorite shirt.
He would routinely talk about how he loved the fit.
The shirt wasn't cheap either.

Nice custom design & high quality.
And there it was.
A grease imprint on it.

I could of easily acted like nothing happened.
But I decided to act like a man...
Or better yet, I decided to act like a teenage boy & tell him what I did.

When I told him, he was visibly irritated.
But was quick to forgive me.

He said, 'Don't worry about it man. You didn't do it on purpose.'

I recall that memory every now and then.
It showed the difference in forgiveness tactics.

And how people process emotions differently.

A nice guy feels emotions like their charismatic counterparts.
But when they forgive, it's not always apparent whether they actually forgave or not.

I didn't know back then **why** I had a kneejerk response to slap my cousin in the van that night.
Nowadays, I do.

It was because of the resentment of continuously getting punched when watching the reality show.

Due to not verbalizing my irritation, the emotions rested in the body.
Then the emotions took up a life of its own.

That's why nowadays, transformational art is becoming a popular concept.
This is when art can be used to process emotions and create value for others in the process.

A nice guy becomes a ticking time bomb because suppressed emotions do not disappear.
Emotions are energy.

Energy cannot be created or destroyed.
Only converted from one form of energy to another.

As I work on the ArmaniTalks brand, and view that lesson of the past with a matured outlook, I realize that nice guys are slowly put to sleep by building communication skills.

'You're saying I have to kill the inner nice guy?'
Yes, that's how **charisma is built.**

That's when the **energy of resentment** is not suppressed.
Instead, it is converted into words.

Either the words can be kept to yourself in a **journal**.
Or the words can be expressed to the cousin who is punching you.

The ticking time bomb happens by those who you least expect it from.
They are quiet.
They are observing.

But you better know...they are feeling.

WHAT IS CREATIVITY?

You ever remembered a dream from the night before?
'Yea, a few times.'
How much of it did you remember?
'Just fragments of it.'

No, I'm talking about remembering most of it. Not just fragments of it.
'Oh in that case, no. I rarely remember most of my dreams.'

For some reason, recently, I have been remembering most of them.
The plot, the context & the characters involved.

One of them from yesterday was when I was calling someone.
I used the feature in the phone where you can speak someone's name & the audio will be recognized by the smart phone.

I used the audio feature because I was driving.
Picture talking to Siri.

As I said the name, **suddenly** the phone begins dialing the wrong number.
That's when things got blurry.
But I recall the number was of someone that I didn't want to call.

That was a moment I remember from the dream.
'So?'
So....

When I woke up:
1. I thought it was a random thing to dream.

2. I realized that the car, the phone, my steering wheel were all made up of my mind.

'So?'
So....

I was watching a tv show a while back.
Noticed how everything looked different.

From the different characters, to the floor they were sitting on, to the lamp in their background.
However, it was all just pixels.
The screen was giving the illusion of differences.

That's when I saw a stunning parallel between a computer/tv screen & the mind.

After getting my masters in information systems, I don't believe I just got an education on technology.
I believe I got an education on perception.

During my classes, I learned how computers worked.
How pixels & audio are all that is needed to give the end user an experience.

Nowadays, when I see someone watching Tv....I look at them and think:

"They are looking at a bunch of pixels & audio. Not the actual people. Yet, they are getting so hyped and excited."

Sort of like when someone is watching a boxing match.
These different pixels & audio are causing the heartbeat to rise, joy to be created & memories to be formed.

There are 2 realities.

- Independent reality.
- Dependent reality.

Dependent reality requires the independent reality to exist.

But the independent reality does not require the dependent reality to exist.

Example...

Back to my dream.

Can the phone from my dream exist without my mind?

'No.'

Why not?

'It's because you were dreaming the phone! You **need** the mind to dream.'

Can my mind exist without the phone from the dream?

'Yea.'

How do you know?

'Because now you are awake. You are writing this email. No dream phone in sight.'

Exactly.

So which one was dependent?

'The phone.'

It was dependent on what?

'Your mind.'

Which one is independent?

'Your mind.'

Damn!

You're smarter than you look.

Now you may be wondering what all this has to do with creativity.

It has a lot to do with it.

The creative mind is not only perceiving the dependent reality.

-It is perceiving the dependent reality while searching for the independent.

^That's the formula for lifelong learning.

Just like the dream showed a bunch of variety, but it was unified by the mind...

And just like the tv showed a bunch of variety, but it was unified by the screen...

There should be something that is unifying life.

It's one thing to say 'yea, I'm sure there is some unifier! Now let me go back to taking a nap.'

That's easy to say.

There are fancy quotes regarding it.

It's different when the intellect is backing up the quote.

When the intellect goes from 'I think there is a unifier' to 'I'm sure there has to be a unifier! And I am going to find it. Where is the independent reality?'

That's the question that unlocks creativity & charges up the mind.

An average mind looks at life & only see's differences.

A creative mind looks at life & only see's connections.

The creative mind is built after aiming to become creative.

It's not just something that happens overnight.

Trial and error is required.

Just like when we dream, we have no clue it's a dream.
Until we wake up.

Likewise, when we are building something, we have no clue it's something unique until looking backwards.

Creativity fuels confident communication.
Without it, you'll always be saying something that has been said.

It's easy to fit in.
It's hard to ask difficult questions & aim to articulate the difficult responses.

CREATING YOUR VOICE

There's a certain beauty to being new to a field.
It's when you are unaware of your deficiencies.

You ever seen someone like that?
Pure raw talent.

This is a person who has drive, hunger & a baseline level of skill.
They are highly moldable.

Although this guy has tons of raw talent, there is still **a lot** of work to be done.
The posture is sloppy, certain movements are lazy & there is minimal understanding of the theory.

Still moldable though.

In a linear world, it's easy to think that the trajectory of this person is UP.
This kid will work hard & get better with time.

'Are you saying that's not the case?'
Sort of. The only direction is not UP. The direction of this fellow includes, up, sideways, back. That's the cost of growth.

In a nonlinear world, this kid will slowly start to become more **problem aware** of his setbacks.
There were certain errors that they were not aware of before.

Before, they didn't think too much before pulling the trigger.
Now there is a small delay before pulling the trigger.

I'll give you an example...

When I first started my YouTube channel, I would just make videos.
Had no clue what I was doing.
Didn't even have products to sell back then.
Just a guy having fun.

One day, I noticed after watching some of my videos, that I didn't blink for certain talks.

I got this advice from another YouTuber that threw me off.
He told me to look directly at the center of the camera.

When I looked at the center of the camera, I noticed I didn't have to blink.
I always thought it was impossible not to blink for a prolonged period of time.
Whenever I would have staring contests with my friends, my eyes would tear up.

So why was it when I was looking at the center of the camera, I didn't have to blink?
I guess this was me learning something new.

I didn't like how I looked when I didn't blink.
This needed to be fixed asap.

For the next video, I was in the zone.
Pure focus.

Then suddenly, I had a thought:
'Yo, did you blink? Blink Armani, blink!'

I entertained that blinking thought for far too long.
This caused me to forget my initial point & I lost track of the video.

When I was pure raw talent, something like this didn't happen.
What the hell?

I have more practice sessions under my belt.
I'm suppose to be getting better.
Why was the blinking issue happening??

It's because we live in a nonlinear world.

Just going UP every single day is not doable.
Somewhere along the lines, the complex system of life holds us back to see if we want it bad enough.

'What did you do with the blinking scenario?'
Once I was problem aware, I let is sit in the back of my subconscious mind.
And gradually, I noticed the blinking issue gradually stop on its own.

Every now and then, it happens again.
Then I make myself problem aware again.
Like a cycle of finetuning...

This is why I've never been a fan of finding your voice.
Because finding is a finite act.

When you find something, it's done.
You don't keep looking.

Creating your voice is an infinite process.

You can do it for life.

Communication skills is a game of the mind.
That's why my newsletter doesn't just talk about speaking.
It also talks about critical thinking, concentrating, building memory etc.

You don't learn all this stuff at once.
You learn it cumulatively, overtime.

Each rep introduces a new problem that may have you thinking:
'Yo wtf? I've been practicing so much. Why am I consistently getting new problems??'

I used to think like that.
Still do every now and then.
That's when I have to check myself.

Without these little problems, I wouldn't be going through a process.
That's what allows me to build my database.

I had a consult call with this guy who told me that he doesn't blink when he is presenting in his Zoom weekly calls.
One of his coworkers bought it up & now he can't stop thinking about it.

What should he do?

I had a data point from my life that I could easily refer to.
I told him to stop actively trying to stare at the computer.
Just look at the general vicinity.
The camera will pick it up & it will look more personable.

Even though him & I didn't end up working together, he said the trick worked beautifully.

Nowadays, his audience members enjoy his delivery and he isn't having to focus so much on where to stare.

This guy has sent me 2 referrals since that initial call.

At the surface level, the 2 referrals seem like something that was given by him.

But for me, the 2 referrals were born from the blinking issue.

What was once an issue is now seen as a gift.

Embrace problems.

You need problems.

Problems are a feature of creating your voice.

Not a bug.

MISTAKE VS MALICE

Imagine you see a 7-foot man walk into a social that you normally host.

You've never seen this 7-foot man before.

How would you break the ice?

You may jokingly say:

'What's the weather like up there?'

I would think that was a harmless question.

But want to know something?

A lot of tall people find that question disrespectful.

A while back, I read 2 Wilt Chamberlain autobiographies.

He was a giant, physically and metaphorically.

He dominated basketball in the 60s and went onto star in some movies.

The 2 books were written decades apart.

One book was written in his 30s.

The other book was written in his 60s.

One thing I noticed about both books was how he bought up his height.

He didn't just talk about it for a few pages.

He spent chapters talking about it.

And he wasn't glowingly talking about it either.

He talked about the **dark parts** of being tall.

He shared how he would routinely have people ask him what the weather was like up there.

Others would a make a game of guessing how tall he was in front of him.

And since he was so huge, he'd often have to duck when going through a door.

If he had to walk through a series of doors in an airport, others would mockingly do the ducking motion behind him.

Think of an average sized person.

There are days they don't want to be seen.

Let's say they have to quickly pick up something from the store.

They wear a big hoodie, go to the store, pick up the item, and come back home.

But for a 7-foot person, that's not always possible.

It's difficult not to be seen.

Wilt gave a funny analogy to drive his point home.

He said that it's socially acceptable for a group to ask a tall person how big his shoes are.

But it's socially unacceptable to ask a fat person:

'Yo, what size pants do you wear?'

Imagine if others made a guessing game out of the fat person's waist size.

I began laughing.

Then I stopped laughing.

I never knew about the pitfalls of being so tall.

The state of KNOWING is what distinguishes a mistake from malice.

-Mistakes are often born from ignorance.

-Malice is born from a sinister intention.

So, if you go to the tall person and break the ice with:
'What's the weather like up there?'

And you genuinely had no clue that tall people find that question disrespectful, then you made a mistake.

But let's say the tall person already notified you that they don't like that question.
However, you ask that question anyways to catch the tall guy off guard.
That was malice.

The inability to distinguish mistakes from malice is why many cut off good people and re-invite snakes back into their life.

It's difficult to spot the difference between a mistake and malice.
It's like trying to read someone's mind.

One place to begin practicing is with yourself.

1. What is one act where you genuinely made a mistake?
2. What is one act where you operated with malice?

The first question is easy to answer.
But for the second question, there is tons of resistance...

PARTNERSHIPS

Today, I'm going to share a story regarding partnerships.

I think the lesson is common sense.

So obvious that I'm going to state it right now..

The lesson in regards to partnerships is to work with someone who has what you lack & you have what they lack.

If you are social, but hate details, then it'll be cutch if you can find a great number cruncher who hates to be social.

Now....

Story time.

Recently, I've been posting small 20 minutes classes on Skillshare.

I diversify a good amount in the ArmaniTalks brand.

Been getting monthly royalties from them.

It's a great platform for creatives.

However, I heard some horror stories of teachers getting their accounts terminated.

Skillshare has a **very** strict content policy.

If you violate their rules 3 times, then you are permanently banned.

I found out that there were people who had huge portfolios of classes that got terminated overnight.

They lost their only stream of income.

My plan for Skillshare was never that.

A 20 minute class requires little effort on my end.

I can do that in my sleep.

Plus, it's just one of my cash flow assets.

No harm in that.

Well, after my public speaking for dummies class posted there, I was issued a content strike & had the video removed.

Apparently, I had one slide showing the entire time on one of the videos.

That's not allowed.

You need **at least** 2 slides per video.

Okay.....

I thought that was it.

I read the rules again to make sure I wasn't missing anything for future content.

When I posted my next class.... I got another strike!

This time, the strike was for having 2 introductions.

But I didn't have 2 intros.

I only had 1.

What gives?

I contacted their support team & they told me that it was because I had an introduction video and an overview video.

Uh...so???

There's no part in the rules that said I couldn't have an overview video.

This was strike 2.

One more & I'm out.

At this point, I was pissed & was like, fuck it.
I'm going to give them a piece of my mind.
In a polite way, of course.

I gently wrote that the rules were not specific. A lot of it was up for interpretation.
After being given a 2nd strike, this made me question whether or not to post another class.

That's all I wrote..

A few days went by.
Then I got an email.

It was an apology from Skillshare Support.
They looked at my video & realized that it satisfied the rules.
And they took the strike off & put the video back up.

I was happy they did this & told them thanks for looking into it.

I found a simple formula that works for me.
1. Create a talking head video.
2. With an introduction slide in the beginning.
3. And a summary slide at the end.
Each video in the classes would follow this simple formula!

I hate editing videos.
This 3 step editing shouldn't take too long, right?

WRONG.

Creating the course is fast as hell.

However, adding in a slide in the beginning & end, adjusting the text, creating summary points, waiting for the video to export etc, ends up taking a LONG time.

A 20 minute video ended up taking over 2 hours to complete!

This whole situation made me realize that I love the creating part.

Video editing though?

I fucking hate it.

Not only with that....

I hate editing thumbnails for YouTube.

Creating graphics on my website.

Or doing anything design related.

That's when I realized, if I am ever going to have a person that I consistently work with, it will be an **artist**.

I want this artist to be so proficient that I do not have to think at all.

I despise visual creative work.

Not my cup of tea.

This was stunning because I'm not the only person like this.

I know plenty of writers who just want to write.

They do not want to touch the cover design of their book, dress up, create a YouTube studio etc.

Those writers in the future will possibly form partnerships with artists.

Normally, when I hear about partnerships in a business context, immediately, I hear phrases like sales, marketing, accounting etc being thrown around.

Rarely do I hear the phrase, 'artist.'

My prediction is as the world becomes more interconnected, more people are going to improve their communication skills for professional & personal reasons.

They will improve speaking, writing, or both.

That's when their mind will MAINLY want to double down on communication skills.

They won't want their mind be dragged to the visual aspects as well.

'How do I learn Photoshop?'

'How do I create a book cover?'

'How do I design a YouTube studio?'

They'll learn how to do the 3 questions I just asked. But I see plenty of them saying:

'Man...I'll do this for now, but I can't wait to outsource this shit.'

Much love to the graphic designers out there.

I built a newfound respect for them.

And the feeling is mutual.

Many graphic designers that I work with have a lot of respect for me.

When I'm done writing a book, and I give it to them to format it ...

A few of them are like:

'You wrote this entire manuscript??'

Hell yea I did.
'That could never be me' they say in a joking way.

I look back at them and think, *'what you're doing could never be me either....my friend.'*

That's when true partnerships are born.

There is a mutual respect between the 2 of you.
Because 1 of you has what the other person lacks & vice versa....

SQUID GAMES

I saw a few posts on Facebook & Twitter recently making fun of Squid Games.

The way the posts were worded, I couldn't tell if the posters were being sarcastic or sharing their honest opinion.

-Watching Squid Games will lower your testosterone.

-Instead of watching tv, do something productive.

-The show is good, but nothing great.

I heard the opinions.

I respected the opinions.

However, when it comes to entertainment & art, I don't take critics seriously.

Their opinions hold little to no value in my world.

I hear what they are saying.

If there is a pattern, I will make a note.

Then I will do my best to consume the art in an unbiased fashion.

The problem with art 'critics' is that they perceive the content from their experiences, not mine.

This can lead to drastically different interpretations.

I believe Rotten Tomatoes has the Interstellar movie rated at a 72%.

72???

The disrespect!

Anything lower than a 99% is outright blasphemy.

But hey, that's just me.

I'm biased towards space movies because I am curious regarding space.

Back to the initial critics who were shitting on Squid Games.

I think some of them were being creatively honest.

I think others were pandering to an algorithm.

They saw that others were talking about the show.

-Demand.

They saw that others were talking highly of the show.

-General consensus.

So a part of them wanted to be different or 'edgy' & decided to change it up with controversial post.

And some of the others probably didn't even watch they show!

They love self improvement so much that the mere idea of watching any form of entertainment is ridiculous to them.

However, they still wanted to put in their 2 cents to let others know they had something to say on the matter.

There are too many components to count.

I never know what behind the scenes motives were present when these critics formed their opinion.

Therefore, I rely on my own judgment.

The less of a group thinker you are, the more you can perceive deeper dimensions in creative works.

This newsletter talks about communication skills.

I believe media plays a large role in communication.

This newsletter is a form of media.

Every email, I have 1-3 people unsubscribe, while I have hundreds of people read it.

Some people hate this newsletter.
Some people love it.

At the end of the day, they are both right...

IDENTITY POLITICS

I had this great interview today with a podcast that deals with crafts work & tools.

It should be up in a few days.

Somewhere in the podcast, the host asked me about people who leave their home country to move to a new place.

How these people must have a sense for adventure and a tolerance for risk.

I think anytime you move somewhere new, you show guts.

It's entering the unknown...

These immigrants who move have a thing called the:

Immigrant's work ethic.

This is a phrase which implies hard work, consistency & staying true to their word.

'Why do you think immigration work ethic exists?'

Because of a reference point.

People who move from a 3rd world country to a 1st world country notice the differences in living standards.

Not only physically, but spiritually.

In a 1st world country, there are tons of opportunities once you fill your mind with knowledge, are disciplined & become more curious.

This sort of immigration work ethic is unlocked when there is a reference point to compare it with.

'What is the reference point?'

Coming from the slums, having dealt with a country with authoritarian rules, or relocating from a country that couldn't even maintain clean streets.

That kind of stuff.

Acknowledging the dark parts makes it easier to appreciate the light.

On the other hand, I see people who have different skin colors, but aren't real immigrants.

They don't have work ethic.

The mind is fascinating.

When you don't give it problems, it creates problems.

There are a lot of entitled people I see.

They talk about how oppressed they are, how they don't have opportunities, and how they are handicapped in life.

While living in a 1st world country!

They have no reference point to ground them & remind them of how great they have it.

Then they go back to using their iPhones, watching garbage content & eating garbage food.

The reason information technology can be dark is due to the battle for power.

That's why identity politics is on the rise.

Where a person's core philosophy is based on the color of skin, rather than character.

Does skin play a role in interactions?

Of course.

(I wrote an email on the role of ethnicities a while back. The post was about how when I was in my masters classes, our teacher would let us organize ourselves into groups. And 9/10 times, the kids would team up with the people who looked like them. It was a primal decision that was made.)

But eventually, for the consciousness to evolve, the identity needs to evolve as well.

I recently saw a viral video of this guy who punched a woman in the subway.
I don't know what happened beforehand.
Think she was reprimanding him for being mean to his kid.

I'm sure she said something along the lines of:
'You need to take a chill pill.'

That's when the video started.
He was rushing to her face, saying:
'Say chill pill again.'

She did.
He punched her dead in the face.

The subway ran amuck with cries of terror.
That's when he said:
'You need to stay out of my black business.'

I think anyone with common sense knows this wasn't a race issue.
However, his mind immediately turned it into a race issue.

I'm sure once this video goes more viral & starts being picked up by mainstream new outlets, they will entertain this encounter as a race issue.

They will have panels talking about the role skin played.
Others will debate this topic.
It will get heated.
Ratings will soar.
Identity politics will be further injected into culture.

Then a group of whining victims will be like:
'Don't you see! Race issues are all around us!!'

There are problems everywhere.
But there are opportunities everywhere as well.

This newsletter is not here to promote more victimhood.
I'm liberal on some stances & conservative on other ones.

I noticed after the man punched the woman...
There was a white man with a baseball cap standing next to that woman..

The person recording this entire incident was saying:
'Damn, her man didn't even defend her when she got punched.'

Wait... the man with the baseball cap is her husband?
And you're just standing there??

I thought there would be some primal instinct to save your woman.
But not for him.
He looked down in terror.

That's why masculinity should not be vilified.

It's raw energy.

Energy that needs to be controlled by good men.

Otherwise, you got men who seem deflated & move scared.

I have no clue if that was her husband.

If it was, it shows that a man should be capable of some sort of violence.

Some form of training.

In his mind, he may think:

'Damn, if I hit this black man & knock him out... What if someone records me & I'm painted to be a racist?'

Or maybe he didn't want to egg the situation on further.

A person who will openly punch a woman in a crowded subway may have a gun or knife on them.

As you can see from this analysis, there are **a lot** of variables to consider.

However, for the identity politics crew, it was all about skin...

The person with an immigrant work ethic is remarkable in another way.

'Which is?'

They don't care if you hate on them. They will move forward anyways.

I'm sure some of the most successful immigrants you know with an accent were mocked by others for their accent.

They didn't cry victim and say:

'Guess I just won't say anything!'

They used it as an opportunity to toughen their thick skin.

And speak even better.

I knew this Sikh who got jumped after the 9/11 debacle.
Others confused him as a Muslim.

He told me the story a couple of years later.
And he had a fire in his eyes when he told that story.
Not fear.
That moment encouraged him to learn to fight mentally &
physically.

-You aren't what happened to you.
-You are what you interpreted of what happened to you.

A tool of the identity politics squad is to weaponize empathy.
They think you need to be accepting of everything, otherwise,
you're a bigot.

No.
Accepting everything means a person lacks principles.

I can't accept a victimhood mindset.
Can't ever condone identity politics here.

'Don't worry Omar, you can't do it because of your skin color.'
False.

Place more focus on the mind.
Feed your mind knowledge that empowers you, not "knowledge"
that makes you think you're missing a leg.

Work hard.
Get tougher through pain.

Never blame the 'man' or 'the system'
Even if they are at a fault.

Allow your mind to take the pressure.
Absorb it.
Develop Picasso like creativity.
Cultivate character that makes you bulletproof.

You truly are unstoppable.

LUCK OF THE DRAW

The Luck of the Draw is defined as:

"Success or failure apparently brought by chance rather than through one's own actions."

For a certain period, I thought this was a quote worth taking seriously.

I took this quote seriously when I lived in Virginia.

During my time in Virginia, my company assigned me to live in a Mansion as I got my training complete.

I lived with a bunch of other people around my age.

Men & women.

Most of them were from Nepal.

They took me in as one of their own.

Even though I was Bengali, they said I look Nepalese.

Eventually, they taught me this one popular card game they would play back at home.

They explained the rules to me, which I pretended like I understood.

Then we began playing.

In the beginning, I was just doing what the kids around me were doing.

Pulling a card and being like 'Ahhh.'

-Sometimes, the 'Ahh' sounded enthusiastic, as if the players got a good card.

-Other times, the 'Ahh' sound deflated, as if the players got a bad card.

My 'Ahh' sounded confused.
As I 'Ahh'd ... I looked around the other players to see if I got a good card or not.

The other players couldn't believe it.
I was getting 1 great card after the next.

That's when my 'Ahh?' turned into 'AHH!!!'
Enthusiasm and pride started to permeate my voice.
I believe I was 24 at the time.
Began believing my own hype with this game.

Imagine the cockiness.
I didn't even understand the rules, but thought I was the man when it came to this game.

Over time, reality started to kick in.
I guess it was a 'Luck of the Draw' moment.
Not true skill.

As years have passed on by, I don't really care for the 'Luck of the Draw' belief.
I think it may work for some people.

However, for me, I don't like to think too much about luck.
I like to think about effort & consistency.
That's what makes me feel good & empowered.

If luck does happen, that's when there is more joy.
It's because I wasn't expecting it.

I made an insight recently where I said:

'Coincidences seem just like coincidence to people who are told about it. But coincidences seem like a magical gift to the person who is experiencing it.'

It's the same with luck.

When it hits me, I'm like:

'Whoa, is this really happening? Awesome! Guess the consistency & work was worth it.'

But when I expect luck, I don't feel good.

I feel 'meh.'

A part of being a lifelong student is constantly reevaluating old beliefs.

Which beliefs serve you.

And which beliefs deflate you?

Just because your 24 self year old believed in something doesn't mean your 40 year old self should.

Allow yourself to grow.

That's when pleasant surprises of luck finds you.

Heart of Gold

Recently, I went to West Palm.
I recall a specific moment that taught me about the value of communication skills.

I'm going to call the 14 year old kid, Hunter.
Picture Hunter to be a family friend of mine.

I was there when Hunter was born 14 years ago.
When he was a baby.

Once Hunter became a few months old, he started to babble.
You know how babies try to talk.

As he got older, he still continued to babble.
Seems to be normal.
Maybe he is still figuring out how to talk.

But as he was hitting 5-8 years old....
He still wasn't speaking.

After doing checkups with the doctors, Hunter was notified to have a speech impediment from autism.

During this trip to West Palm, I was sitting on my couch watching a Netflix show.

As I'm sitting on the couch, Hunter plops right next to me.
Then he starts showing me a clip of the Alvin & the Chipmunks movie.
I believe it was the trailer.

He kept repeating this one scene, **over and over again.**
This is the part where there is a man who is yelling out:
'ALVINN!!!'

Hunter kept rewinding to that scene.
He was looking at me to see my reaction.

After replaying the same scene for the 10th time, that's when I asked:
'Why are you keep showing me this scene?'

He started laughing.
And he rewinded back to the scene:

Alvin!!!!
Rewind.

Alvin!!!!
Rewind.

Alvin!!!!
Rewind.

I had no clue what he was trying to tell me.
Why was this scene so captivating for him?
I saw nothing.

But that's when I realized...
He wouldn't be able to tell me why that scene was important.

The ArmaniTalks brand predominantly covers communication skills.

The short stories teach speaking & writing skills to better handle yourself in the real world.

What I noticed from this incident was the reverse.
Where communication skills seize to exist.

I think building a Heart of Gold means:
The ability to give & empathize skillfully.

There is skill to the act of giving.
There is skill to the act of empathizing.

I used to think the way to build empathy was thru the process of addition.
Where you need to gain a certain experience to see another point of view.

However, nowadays, I believe empathy is built through the process of subtraction, then addition.

This is why a person who is healthy doesn't care too much.
But when they are not healthy...
They hate it.
-Subtraction.

Then when they are given the health back (hopefully), they are grateful.
-Addition.

Through this subtraction-addition process, they can now perceive a new lens when they see someone else going through a similar scenario.

During the moment with Hunter, I did not lose my ability to communicate.

But I was able to see what it's like when you cannot articulate what you are thinking.

In a lapse, I saw myself not being able to write or speak either.
And in the next lapse, I realized that I could write & speak.
That's when subtraction & addition led to a burst of empathy for Hunter's scenario.

He is an enthusiastic kid.
I will give him that.
Always running around & burning calories.
Slowly, he is stringing words together.

To build a heart of gold, it's about accumulating these loops of life.

Subtraction
Addition.
Perspective shift.

Subtraction.
Addition.
Perspective shift.

Multiple perspective shifts lead to a new paradigm.
A new worldview.

The world is not fixed.
The world is in a state of becoming.

It's becoming a world where more experiences are being geared to help people gain these perspective shifts on their own.

So, one day they will be able to:

-Give with skill.
-Empathize with skill.

Tactical empathy is a real thing.
It prevents you from being manipulated & acting like an idiot.
Also, it prevents you from being cold & too logical.

CONTAGIOUS ATTITUDE

Ageism is defined as:
"Prejudice or discrimination on the grounds of a person's age."

Often, when I used to think of ageism, I thought of discrimination towards an elderly person.
A young person probably said:
'What can Sue do? She's too old!'

But I've noticed a reverse too.
Where young people are discriminated in certain fields.
'What could this young fella possibly know? He has barely hit puberty!'

While this young fellow is 25 years old.
Not too old.
But not too young either.

Young people often have an awkward transition period in corporate life.
Where the young buck is figuring out how to add value in a professional setting.

I'm not going to talk about others.
But I'll talk about my experience in corporate life.

I've worked in a variety of different fields.
Aerospace, IT & the finance departments.

What I saw was surprising.
'What was that?'
Walking zombies.

Tons of workers who have been in a company for a long time hated it.

They lacked enthusiasm.

The highlight of their day was to gather around one another & gossip.

Often, the only way to bond with these folks was to gossip yourself.

But what if you didn't want to gossip?

Then the potential subject matters to converse about would drastically reduce.

This is where primal value comes in clutch.

Enthusiasm.

A person with a 'can do' attitude is a Rockstar.

Others want to see what the hype is about.

Why is this person so enthusiastic for??

A large part of being enthusiastic is being self motivated.

Because when you look around you, most individuals don't have that fire.

That's not a personal attack.

It is what it is.

The enthusiastic spirit is capable of keeping the spirits high DESPITE the environment.

If this person is looking at the environment to feel fire, then they will become volatile.

The volatility will make them jaded over time.

Therefore, there needs to be SOMETHING that's causing the inner fire to be lit.

And that 'something' is best kept a **secret**.

Having that 1 secret to yourself never hurts.

Be giving with other types information, sure.

But have at least 1 thing solely for yourself.

It's great when this secret is empowering rather than draining.

A draining secret is one where you killed someone before, but got away with it.

Even if you never tell someone else, your gloomy face will imply something suspect.

An empowering secret is a vision that you're taking incremental steps towards.

Even if you never tell someone else, your face will have a glow to it.

That's the way of an enthusiastic spirit.

This is **primal value** that adds life to a floor of walking zombies.

INFINITE INTELLIGENCE

One of the soft skills covered by the ArmaniTalks brand is creativity.

The goal is to break down creativity in a systematized way where any bubba can understand it.

Today, I want to talk about the concept of infinite intelligence. The ability to perceive infinity.

When I used to hear the saying:
"We are infinite beings having a finite experience."
I scoffed at it.

A part of me would get annoyed with these types of comments. Mainly because I couldn't perceive it.

Later on, after starting ArmaniTalks, I started to have a shift in mindset.
It comes down to identification.

I believe I have created over 1000 of these daily newsletters. Time flies!

Also, I've written over 40,000 tweets, made many YouTube videos discussing a variety of ideas and much more.

The more I keep thinking I'll be running out of ideas, the more ideas I get!

When transitioning from the physical domain to the mental, I came to realize that ideas really are infinite.

It's *impossible* to run out.

This is the golden era of creativity.

I'm very optimistic.

The more ideas I created, the more I realized it came down to identification.

Normally, a person starts off identifying only with their body.

The smarter they get, the more they begin identifying with their mind.

'I'm so well read! You didn't read that book? Let me tell you about it,' the mega mind thinks.

Then they subconsciously judge the mental peasant for not being as well read as them.

It's 2 humans interacting.

-1 identifies more with their body,

-1 identifies more with their mind.

Most people stop there.

Another sphere is identifying more with awareness.

The **observer** of the mind & body.

In my **introspection for dummies video**, I gave a mental cheatcode to introspect with EASE.

Rather than identifying with the mind & body...

Say:

"I have a mind and body."

This creates a micro separation in terms of identification & makes it easier to introspect & gain insights at will.

As I got older, I saw why people said stuff like: "We are infinite beings having a finite experience." They probably identified more with awareness and used the mind and body as a tool.

That was one idea.

Recently, I have been thinking about a flashback moment of creating a radio in college.

I had a professor named Dr. Wiley who kept babbling about the theory of building a radio.

He talked about the electromagnetic spectrum, sender, receiver, breadboards etc.

This man spent months talking about the theory.

I thought:

'Shut the fuck up & let me build the damn radio already, old man!'

After months of this goober babbling away, he finally allowed us to build the radio.

I got the breadboard, used the others parts in my lab kit & followed a few basic rules.

After days of tinkering, I got the radio to work!

It was able to tune into frequencies from around the area.

I was amazed.

'What did you find so amazing about it?'
I found it amazing because I was tuning into information.

Invisible information was floating all around me.
It was just a matter of creating the right resonation with this radio & tuning into the right frequency.

Nowadays, when I practice something, I have 2 perceptions that I wrestle with.

1 perception is:
Practice & build neural pathways.

Another perception is much more profound.
It's viewing the human as a walking radio.

This is where an **infinite sea** of potential is all around us.
Practice so you create the right neural pathways to tune into the infinite energy & allow it to flow through you.

What if there is a potential in the infinite space where driving already exists...
And the neural pathways firing and wiring during practice sets the correct combination to effectively tune into that space?

That's why learning something & doing it on autopilot fascinates me.
Turn an act into an instinct.

If someone gives me a Rubik's cube, my palms automatically solve it.

It's so autopilot to a point, where if I disrupt the autopilot process by thinking, I can't solve the Rubik's cube!

It's as if there is static being created like a distorted radio song.

I just need to let it be in my palms & it will solve itself.

That's because I've solved the Rubik's cube over 5,000 times & the neural pathways are set.

Similar to typing.

If I think too much about the letters, then my fingers fuck up and I can't write properly.

Instead, I have the vision in my mind & the fingers just flow automatically.

In the Eastern side of the world, the view of reality is drastically different than the West.

There is no such thing as empty space.

A seed does not grow into a tree.

A tree already exists as potential in the seed, which THEN grows into a tree.

This is known as involution.

The predecessor to evolution.

The senses are easily capable of being fooled.

When you are looking at a movie of Titanic...

You're not looking at the real Leonardo DiCaprio.

You're actually looking at pixels & hearing audio waves.

But that's not even accurate!

You're actually seeing the byproduct of processing magnetrons, circuity & electricity creating ON/OFF, ON/OFF signals.

That's how easily the senses can be fooled.

It's perceiving an entirely different thing to be something else.

Just because the senses see empty space does not make that accurate.

From the context of a radio, there is no empty space.

It's information.

To relay information, 2 things are required.

Message & the medium.

The message is the song.

The medium is the illusion of empty space.

For this newsletter, the message is my insight on infinite intelligence.

The medium is the email platform that I can write on.

Anyways, this was a quick talk on creativity & seeing the infinite potential in things.

This newsletter is not meant to get others to agree with me.

Instead, it's to get people pondering on bigger questions.

During Nikola Tesla's time, he was pondering on telecommunications.

In his era, talking about wireless communication was ridiculous! It seemed like a fantasy.

Others looked at him like a weirdo.

However, he got his mind absorbed in something **big.** This created new thought waves & from that, Tesla's inventions still live on to this day.

While his haters are forgotten.

Rather than worrying about a mean comment someone said to you 5 years ago.

Start thinking about BIG, GRAND possibilities.

This is how you become a creative genius & a walking, talking idea machine.

DIFFERENT FACES

Recently, I ordered a microphone from Amazon.
They delivered it to the wrong house.

I called their customer support to notify them of the issue.
Immediately, they sent a new microphone.

I received the new microphone & noticed it was not compatible with a software that I was working with, so I decided to return it.

The return process began a month ago.
There was a man at the UPS who scanned my package & said:
'You're all set.'

A part of me wanted to ask for a receipt.
Another part of me noticed he said 'you're all set' with so much confidence that asking for a receipt was not worth it.

So I thanked him and left.

As a few weeks went by, it still showed 'return started' on Amazon.
This was unusual. Normally, when a refund starts, it's competed in a matter of days. Few weeks is stretching it.

Once the weeks turned into months, I called back Amazon support.
This time, it was a lady named Inca who picked up. She was enthusiastically trying to solve the problem.

Once I got off the phone, I felt confident.
Now it's definitely resolved!

As a few days go by, I received an email stating that I'm now being asked to return the Microphone which was never delivered to my crib!
Otherwise, I'll be charged in my credit card.
Huh???

I called them back again & spoke even slower.
And this time, the issue got resolved.

'You must hate Amazon customer support, right??'
Not at all.
In fact, I think they are top notch.

Each time I got on call with them, the person did their best to help me out.
That's why I always respect Amazon. They know how to keep the priorities the priorities.

Now flip this with when I was a SELLER on Amazon.
I still sell books on Amazon to this day.

But back in the days, I used to sell tumblers, superhero cellphone cases, Bluetooth beanie's etc.

Running a business on Amazon in 2015 was the Wild, Wild West.
Different people getting fake reviews.
Poor quality items with 'awesome' customer feedback.
Everything was loose.

Overtime, Amazon started to get more strict.

They would take off reviews.

They would randomly terminate seller account's.

They would randomly do a whole bunch of other hoopla.

My business partner, Tom, & I thought there was nothing to worry about.

We were doing everything ethically.

I was the big vision guy.

Tom was the details oriented guy.

He read the Amazon rules a few times & let me know there was nothing to worry about from our end.

However, life hits.

Business is a game of continuously solving problems.

One time, our supplier in China accidentally put the gray tumblers in the red tumblers box & but the red tumblers in the gray tumblers box.

Soon, we were being flooded with refund requests.

Amazon put a flag on our listing.

Great....

I call my supplier in China, Andy, and asked him what the hell happened.

He notified me of the issue and said he would fix it asap.

He just needed to have Amazon sell the units back or he could refund us.

Tom & I decided to go with the refund.

However, we had another problem on our hands.

'What?'

Getting the swapped items discarded from the warehouse.

Not only was it the Wild Wild West for sellers, it was also just as bad for their customer support.

Tom & I both got on the phone & called their support.

What proceeded was one of the most annoying moments from my life.

Okay, I'm probably exaggerating, but it was pretty bad.

Tom & I had to keep repeating what happened & what we needed done.

That's when a representative would be like:

'I'm sorry this happened to your sir. But my team cannot solve this problem. Let me transfer you to the team who can.'

We got transferred.

Then the new representative would be like:

'Hello, my name is Mike. How may I help you?'

So we had to explain the WHOLE situation over again.

Explaining the situation seems like an easy thing...

But it's not.

Because each time you are explaining it to another person, each time you need to adjust your delivery.

It's like explaining pre calculus to someone who knows algebra, someone who knows calculus, and someone who knows geometry.

Each one is different.

Days turned into weeks.

Weeks turned into months.

And the problem became a pain in the ass.

We were eventually able to solve it.

This moment showed the **stark contrast** of the experience I had as a customer vs a seller.

I get Amazon.

It's a game of Different Faces.

Different faces is the concept that 'authenticity' is rarely fully accurate from the way the traditional mind sees it.

'How does the traditional mind see it?'

Authenticity is viewed as when a person is acting the same way with everyone.

"Ah, Jim...That's an authentic man right there! He acts the same way with everyone! You will never catch Jim acting differently."

There are a few people like Jim who really do act the exact same with everyone.

But I don't think that's the norm.

I think the norm is that different people wear different faces with different people.

Not in a, *'snake like way'*.

But more so in an, *'enhanced delivery like way.'*

-A powerful lawyer can suddenly flip to doing baby talk with his new newborn.

-A person who is shy off camera, knows how to flip the SWITCH when playing her acting role.

-A kid talks differently to her friend vs her mom.

You get the point.

By having a dynamic view of the personality, it becomes easier to reshape one's view of 'authenticity.'

Being the same with everyone may sound good on paper.

But I don't think it's always good in practice.

Sometimes, you'll have to listen more.

Sometimes, you'll have to speak more.

Sometimes, you'll have to do a blend of both.

Different faces is bad when the intent is corrupt.

But different faces is a social superpower when being hyper aware of the context.

GREAT TEACHERS

There are positions designed for great teachers.

Sometimes, the person doesn't even have to teach.

They just need to be able to explain things clearly.

In the author's preface of my book, Speak Easy...

I talk about how at one point, I was being invited to engineering meetings that I didn't belong in.

These were meetings with higher ups & the main players.

I was barely even a junior engineer at the time!

Why?

It was **because** I was a junior engineer.

 I was still moldable.

I had enough technical knowledge to be competent. But not too much technical knowledge to sound like a robot.

This allowed me to speak clearly to the stakeholders about updates.

On the other hand, the senior engineers would make things complex.

They would talk about the excessive details that would confuse people with limited technical knowledge.

The ability to explain things clearly led to more visibility at work.

Explaining things clearly comes down to knowing that others just want to know what's important.

No need to prove how smart you are.

This is difficult.

When a person is talking about themselves, it releases the same pleasure as having sex.

And when a person is speaking about something they KNOW, it feels like they are talking about themselves.

This is when the subject being discussed becomes a part of the subject discussing it.

The ability to explain things clearly requires emotional intelligence and restraint.

It comes down to intuitively knowing:

'Just because it's important to me does not mean the other person should know it.'

Overtime, people who can explain things clearly become a coveted social presence.

Especially when deadlines need to be met & pressure is through the roof.

At one point or another, you may be called to explain things CRYSTAL clear.

Get a head start by creating an Articulation Chamber in your home & practicing this fine art.

In the Speak Easy Book, I introduce you to innovative concepts to improve your communication skills.

You'll learn:

-How to take your voice to the gym.

-How to build an interesting personality to create compelling ideas on autopilot.

-And how to network with others without being a scumbag.

VALUE OF PATIENCE

A few days ago, I had a meeting with the driver's license department.

It was in regards to renewing my vehicle registration.

However, the person I dealt with said that something was wrong with my driver's license.

Therefore, I had to go to another department.

The lady gave me the other department's contact information & showed me how to book an appointment.

When I attempted to book, they were packed.

Thursday at 12:15 pm was the earliest date.

Which was today.

I went there pretty early.

There was a short lady in front of me in the check-in line.

She had brown hair and was wearing a mask.

She got checked in.

Then I got checked in right after her.

After checking in, I looked for a chair.

It was busy!!

I ended up sitting next to the lady who was in front of me a few minutes earlier.

We both sat & glazed at the tv...

The others in the waiting room glazed at the tv too....

One by one, the ticket numbers were being called:
"J1239"
"J1240"
"A492"
"G204"

I had no clue what kind of pattern they were following.
But what I did know was that my ticket number was J1265.

Initially, I thought I was going to be at the location for 20 minutes. I was planning to be in & out.
Especially considering how I made an appointment earlier!!

However, my plans were foiled.

15 minute passes.
30 minute passes
1 hour passes...

I have this habit of shaking my right leg when I am sitting.
-Sometimes, I do it because I am getting impatient.
-Other times, I do it because it's quite soothing.
Today, I was doing it because it was soothing.

The lady next to me see's me shaking my leg..
I think she thinks I'm getting impatient.

That's when she starts shaking her leg too.
She starts shuffling.
And starts sighing more.

Her body language insinuates she is getting agitated.
Her body language is also implying:

'What the hell is taking so long?? I made an appointment already!'

I know her number was J1264 because she was standing right in front of me.

At this point, we have something in common.

I stopped shaking my leg.

I think it was making her nervous.

Humans have mirror neurons that subconsciously picks this stuff up.

After restraining my leg, I wanted to do something.

Sitting aimlessly like that was boring.

The tv was playing a cooking show.

But the recipes were not interesting.

It was granola & a bunch of that nasty crap.

So I sat there & started to exercise my memory.

I play this mind game where I practice my concentration skills.

I recall information from my past, and try to recall it to clarity.

Now I was feeling entertained again.

1.5 hours passes on by.

And they are only on ticket J1245.

I'm ticket J1265.

The lady next to me was now fidgeting more than ever.

You could tell she was boiling with rage with how long it was taking.

It's like the ticket monitor was teasing us too.

Every time it was J12...something.
It'd switch to a brand new letter out of nowhere!

Like A204.
G495.
And we wouldn't see the J's for a while.

After 2.5 hours were up, J1264 was finally called.

The lady sprung up.
And she gave me a look like:
'We made it.'
Shortly after, I was called as well.
I got up.
We made made it....

One thing I have realized with Soft Skills is that it's often in these mundane moments where you have the opportunity to work on these skills.
This was a moment of exercising patience.

It's easy to exercise patience when we are supposed to exercise patience.
It's hard to exercise patience when it's an unfair scenario.
Today, I experienced the latter.

Because I booked the appointment.
Came early.
Still had to wait that long.

The narrative mind was like:
'What the fuck, this isn't fair.'

To take it a level further, the reason my license was giving a problem was due to a technical issue on their end.

No fault of my own.

After I got out, the guy who handled my ticket said:

'Sorry about that again!'

So it made the narrative mind be like:

'This really, really, really isn't fair. Now you should lash out!'

When the narrative mind is like that, that's when it's the best time to exercise patience.

Because that's when the internal world gets the most worked out.

Getting that workout is not easy.

In my case today:

-I was calm.

-Jittery.

-Bored.

-Entertained.

To the outside world, I'm just sitting.

In the inside world, I'm practicing emotional intelligence.

Soft skills isn't always glitz and glam.

Where you are having an army of people watching you give a speech.

A lot of soft skills is built from the unsexy.

And one of the unsexy traits is patience.

If you're still reading, a part of you may resonate with this story.

I'm sure you experienced something similar at one point.

Build soft skills when it's not glamorous.

CHANGING MINDS

I'm happy that I started ArmaniTalks in 2018 rather than 2012.
I used to be a completely different person.

Not only different in terms of looks.
But also different in terms of ideas.

For a while, I was very much on the liberal side.
I would often look for YouTube videos of guys like Sean Hannity, Bill O'Reilly & Megyn Kelly losing debates.
If they lost or were close to losing, that'd make me feel happy.

I used to think:
'How could anyone possibly think like these people??'

As a few years went by, I started my first business.
When I started this business, something happened.
'What?'
I started to change my mind.

It's not like I suddenly agreed with everything they said.
However, I was able to **understand** where they came from.

Before, I couldn't understand at all.
But now... I could see *flashes* of the points they were making.

Just like that, I was introduced to what it's like to change your mind.
It happens gradually until it happens SUDDENLY.

The ArmaniTalks content is advice to my younger self.

This does 2 things:

1. It keeps the content in a constant state of evolution.

2. It prevents me from being some sort of preacher.

1. Evolution

I don't like to identify with too many things.

I consider myself a lifelong learner.

By not identifying with many things, it's easier to not personalize ideas.

The less personal, the more I can explore.

If I see the need to discard an old model of thinking, I'll be the first one to do it.

2. It prevents me from being some sort of a preacher

It's called ArmaniTalks.

Not Armani Tells you What to do.

I think the best changes come from inspiration.

Especially in a field like communication skills.

That's why a lot of the content I produce are anecdotes.

Where the lesson is up for interpretation.

When the lesson is up for interpretation, it leads to more profound changes for the reader because it bypasses logic.

-Hard skills is learned by utilizing logic.
-Soft skills is learned by perceiving beyond logic.

ONE experience can come out of nowhere & alter your perception of reality.

And you never know when it will happen.

That's why I think being humble is not only smart for empathy reasons.

Also, it prevents you from looking like a jackass.

You know those ideas that you despise a lot?

Make sure you are being more curious about it.

Human are **recruiters.**

They want you to join their side.

Some people will get minimal understanding on a field & they will parade around like they know everything.

They'll accidentally spread misinformation with a snobby attitude causing others to resent that field.

And this can cause you to get a negative perception of a field which deserves respect!

Let me give you an example.

A few years ago, I had a disgusted attitude towards p90X.

This is a **90 day work out program.**

The reason I had this disgusted attitude towards it was because there were 2 brothers I knew who kept hyping it up.

They kept saying:
'Trust me, you need to ditch the gym & do p90x. It's totally worth it!'

Then I looked at these 2 brothers.
Fatter than the year before.

How were they saying this program worked when they were looking more out of shape?

These 2 brothers would tweet a lot & would be vocal about their workouts.

Eventually, p90x became a joke in our community .
We thought of it as a workout program that made you fatter.

Fast forward 2 years.
I decide to give the program a chance with one of the fat brother's.

As I did the program, I immediately noticed how awesome it was!
It was a complete plan that covered workout, diet and sleep.

Within a few months, I started to notice gargantuan changes in my body.
I was amazed!

'What about the other fat brother you were working out with?'
He stayed the same.

I learned that he would do the working out part well.
But he wouldn't diet properly.

The man would eat a box of Oreo's right after a workout.
Followed by a few McDoubles.

No wonder this buffoon wasn't getting results!!
His fat brother was the same.
He once told me:
'Armani, I only ate 1 tub of ice cream today.'

A tub?
Fool, why would you eat that much?!
Show some damn discipline for the 90 days.
Or at least reduce your input.

It made me livid because these guys were the poster boy's for p90x.
But they were NOT properly executing the program.

I wonder how many people were turned off from p90x due to the 2 brothers..
They probably told their friends who were considering the program:
'Trust me, p90x doesn't work. I know 2 people who have gotten fatter from doing it.'

This is how it works with knowledge too.
You give someone a tad bit of information, and they act like they know it all.

Then they parrot the information with poor understanding & turn others off from it.
Be able to spot these people..

You're only one experience away from potentially shifting your worldview forever.

Be humble
Be a lifelong learner.
And avoid the temptations of being a jackass.

CONFIDENCE IRONY

In 2010, I went to West Palm Beach for the Asian Food Fair.

This is an event where multiple Asian ethnicities get together in a fair to eat, watch dances and socialize.

There was a kid named Jim who had a big van & was picking up the kids who needed a ride.

He picked up 5 kids, my brother & me.

All the other passengers lived in West Palm Beach.

But I was the only guy from Tampa visiting.

Once I got in the car, they all started talking about events that happened in West Palm.

And I felt out of the loop.

-The people they were talking about...I had no clue who they were.

-The events they were talking about... I had no clue what they were.

I was looking for something to contribute on.

As I was waiting.

The guy who picked us up, Jim...

Decides to call me out.

He's like:

'Damn Armani, you think you're too good for us or something? How come you're not saying anything?'

Before giving me a chance to respond, he continues his diatribe.

'That's what happens. When people move from West Palm, they come back acting like someone new.'

There was this kid named Saad who was sitting next to Jim in the passenger seat nodding his head.

I knew Jim.

But I had no clue who the fuck Saad was.

Why the hell was he nodding his head acting like he knew me??

Jim continues talking.

At that point, my brother jumps in and says:

'Yo man, drop it. You guys are talking about topics he doesn't even know about.'

I'm glad he had my back.

Whenever someone has your back when you're ganged up on…it feels good.

When we got to the event, there was tension.

It felt like me vs Jim & his minions.

He pretty much painted me as the guy who thought he was too good for people.

So the others in the car were talking to me like they **believed** the narrative.

I could tell by their body language & how they kept excusing themselves.

Screw them!

During that moment, I learned how easy it was to fool people.

Minds are highly moldable.

Someone just needs to say something with conviction, and others are like:

'He does have a point you know.'

Nowadays, I am grateful for that moment because it led me to create a concept called the Confidence Irony.

The Confidence Irony is when:

-We amplify someone else's confidence while simultaneously undermining our own confidence.

This mindset leads to getting offended quicker & not being able to read body language.

Much better to flip it.

View yourself as confident while viewing the other person as not confident.

Now you're thick skinned & much more composed.

No clue what got into Jim that day.

But I think he had a few people switch up on him once they moved.

So when I got in the car, he elevated my confidence levels so high, that he viewed me as snobby.

Not knowing that I was nervous because I was trying to find a topic to relate to the West Palm passengers with.

That's what caused tension for both of us.

Had he flipped it...

And framed himself as the confident one while I wasn't as confident...

Then he may have thought:

'Oh wait, Armani hasn't been in West Palm for some time. He can't contribute to these topics. How about I bring up something that will allow him to participate?'

I have been guilty of violating the Confidence Irony many times in my life too.

This caused me to perceive something as disrespect when I shouldn't have perceived it that way.

It's never too late to learn the Confidence Irony & implement it.

Watch your patience rise & judgment melt.

OPINIONS & MONEY

Give a bubba a formula & the bubba will take advantage.
One example is the Feedback Sandwich.

A feedback sandwich is a systematized way to give criticism.
Open with what the person did right - **Bun***.*
Talk about what they did wrong & how they can improve - **Meat**
Reinforce what they did right - **Bun**

This sandwich makes it easier to have your message heard.
Much better than opening with the criticism.

Now the bubba feels like they have been given a key to a new world.
They start critiquing people left and right!

They critique their waitress.
They critique family members.
And they critique friends.

Eventually, others get fed up with the bubba's behavior & distance themselves from him.
It's because people don't like being critiqued if they didn't ask.

Every now and then, it's fine.
But too much criticism leaves a poor taste in their mouth.

Even if you are someone who doesn't behave like this towards others...
Others may behave like this with you.

What happens when YOU are incessantly being criticized by other bubbas?

How do you behave?

I have a framework for this.

My framework is to view opinions as money.

I can clearly distinguish between a penny & a 100 dollar bill.

However, with opinions, it becomes blurrier.

Without viewing opinions as money, all opinions will seem important.

Especially the mean ones.

'Should I view mean opinions as worth less & good opinions as worth more?'

No.

Don't see mean or nice.

Assess it in terms of value.

To assess value, there needs to be some kind of goal that you're progressing on.

If someone is giving you weight loss tips when you're bulking, then immediately, the opinion can be seen as less valuable.

Because it is contradicting the goal.

Without the goal...

Fat, skinny, maintenance, are all the same!

Sometimes, your haters will give you the best feedback.

The ArmaniTalks brand doesn't talk about anything divisive or political.

So I don't get many haters.

But every now and then, I do.

When I get a hater, I don't block them.

Instead, I try to see if they are saying anything I should listen to.

Plenty of times, they noticed something about me that allowed me to level up.

In this case, a hater gave me a more valuable opinion than a 'yes man.'

When I view opinions as money, I personalize less.

In the real world, I don't get angry that I cannot buy much with a penny.

I just accept it and go about my day.

When I make the mental note that a certain opinion (at this point in my life) is worth a penny...

I don't make a big fuss.

I just go about my day.

So the next time you're sweating opinions for too long..

Simply ask:

-Am I being the fool who is stepping over a dollar to pick up a dime...simply because it's more shiny?

OR

-Am I the winner who knows how to distinguish dimes from dollars?

PRIMAL WEALTH

The concept of wealth is a subject that has a lot of interpretations.
I've noticed different groups of people offer different perspectives on the matter.

Spiritual people say that money is energy.
Technical people say that money is the numbers on a screen.

Different ways of looking at the same thing.

I view money as connected knowledge.
Actually, I view most of life that way.

I recall one time I was reading a book as a kid, and I felt a strong sensation in my chest.
This was a book called Brute Force.

I thought:
'Whoa, this book must have some sort of power! I need to tell others.'

I told a few of my classmates about Brute Force.
And one of them responded back with:
'I hate that book! You can't pay me to read that again!!'

I was shocked.
How could we have such different interpretations??

Although I didn't know it at the time, I was being introduced to what value was.

Value is not something *out there.*

Value is something *in here.*

The reason I liked the book was because I felt emotions from it.
Those emotions indicated value to me.

The reason my classmate didn't like the book was because they didn't feel any emotions from it!

At the end of the day, the book remained the same.
Objectively, it was a collection of papers, letters & a cover.
Subjectively is where the value was assigned.

A few years later, one of my friends was playing a Kevin Hart stand up special.
And I don't know what it was...
But I didn't find that stand up funny at all.

I was with a group.
They were laughing their asses of.
And I was puzzled because I didn't see what was so funny.

We were all looking at the same screen.
However, the interpretations were vastly different.

This was something that my technical side didn't want to see.
I didn't like the concept of 'feelings'.
Due to how ambiguous feelings were & how difficult it was to quantify.

But there was no way I could runaway from it when I was entering Toastmasters.

In one of my first ever Table Topics, I was given the topic:
'Waffle Stompers.'

I had no clue what the word meant.

And that was the point!

The goal was to create a speech of what I thought the word meant.

So I created a short talk saying that a Waffle Stomper is someone who stands outside Waffle House & stomps on other people's food.

There were a few of the audience members who started laughing.

One of them was laughing louder than the others.

When I saw that my random string of words incited laughter, once again, I saw that feelings were some how involved in measuring value.

Afterwards, one of the veteran members came to me and was like:

'Hey man, you did a great job. I know you're not a member of this club yet...But guests rarely participate. Your impromptu speech made my mood better.'

Hm...

It made your mood better?

That's when I started to realize a concept known as Primal Wealth.

The ability to create feelings in others.

Rather than trying to make someone feel a certain way.

My goal is to feel that way first & display the emotion.

And others feel it as a byproduct.

This is where communication skills becomes powerful.

The first step required is thick skin.

If the guy who wrote Brute Force was butthurt because my classmate hated it...
Then he'd filter himself more to appeal to my classmate.
While completely ignoring how I liked it!

To be a better communicator & create feelings in others, it's best to assume you can never appeal to everyone.

This is an important step because it allows for more authenticity in terms of delivery.

When the desire to appeal to everyone has fallen away...
That's when you're talking to half the people.
And from the half, even less of them will **physically** feel the sensations of the words.

It's that way with any content.

In the information age, the world becomes more interconnected.
In the process of this interconnection, more people are going to be creating content of some sort.
It's just a matter of time in my opinion.

The content will not always be on youtube, emails, tweets etc.
It can also be something like creating a training video at work.

It's smart to be 5 steps ahead while others are thinking on a day by day basis.

To get a head start on what it's like to build primal wealth...
Simply ask yourself:

'What already makes me feel a certain feeling without much intellectual thought?'

It can be a certain YouTuber you follow, a certain newsletter, you read, a certain friend you are around etc.

By understanding the feelings in your body, it becomes easier to influence the feelings in someone else's body.

CHOOSING SIDES

I've had a lot of fallouts in the past.
I've seen a lot of people have fallouts in the past.

A fallout is a disagreement between parties which no longer allows them to continue the relationship.
Think about it real quick...

Remember the people you were really cool with a few years ago?
How many of them are you still cool with today?

Some of those relationships faded away.
Nothing malicious.

While other relationships abruptly ended because snake moves were involved.

When a fallout happens, people want to vent.
They want to tell their respective circles about how the other person did them wrong.

Then their respective circles say stuff like:
-You were definitely in the right!
-I never liked Frankie either.
-What a jerk!

Pretty much believing the entire story that their fellow peer is delivering.

I've learnt from personal experience that choosing sides isn't always smart.
But this is a **gray** topic.

Let me illustrate with an example.

John & Susie.
They were dating.
Everything was going well.

One day, John & Susie decide to break up.
John goes to **his** friends and tells them how Susie was in the wrong.
Susie goes to **her** friends & tells them how John was in the wrong.

Each parties circle takes their respective friends side.
Anything wrong with that?
Probably not...

But let's imagine if John & Susie had the **same** friend circle before dating.
Now when they break up, the stakes have risen!

Friendships often get broken apart when a relationship falls apart.

This is when learning how NOT to take a side is smart.
Especially before getting both sides of the story.

You'll be surprised how often people mess this up.
They'll often believe the person who sounds more believable.

Often, one party may not want to badmouth the other, while the other party *has to* vent.
This again paints another social variable.

Let's say John wants to vent.

But Susie wants to move on.

Just because Susie doesn't defend herself does not show guilt.
It shows that she has other priorities.

Learning how NOT to have an opinion is a skill.

-Especially when others are constantly trying to convince you why it's <u>smart</u> to have an opinion on the matter.
-Or why it's <u>irresponsible</u> to not have an opinion on the matter.

In the social skills world, learning how NOT to take a side is a skill.

Just because there are 2 sides does not mean you have to lean a certain way.

The middle ground territory often allows a person to see the bigger picture.

Remember how the famous saying goes...

There are 3 sides to a story.
John's side.
Susie's side
And the truth.

STRATEGIC FAITH

There are certain phrases that create images in the mind.
And the images aren't always pleasant.

One of those unpleasant images are created with the word 'faith.'
It may create the mental image of an unhinged person.

A person who scoffs at logic.
Is worshipping superstitions.
And is probably not a smart guy.

But that's blind faith.
The type of faith that is built on no form of evidence.

It's difficult to always have evidence in the real world.
Heck, innovation is born DESPITE not having evidence!

Rather than blind faith, I'm a proponent of Strategic Faith.
Similar concept with blind risks vs strategic risks.

I'm not a big fan of heights.
Also, not a big fan of doing 'extreme sports.'

Riding a motorcycle for example.
Or skydiving.
Why would I do that?

I don't have much desire to educate myself on those fields.
Nah, I'll pass.

I don't hate on people who do those activities.

But for me, that's not strategic risk.

It's just risk.

My idea of strategic risk is doing something that I have more control over.

Like starting a business.

Is there a lot of volatility with a business?

Yes.

But it's impossible to have 0% volatility in anything.

Just gotta' decide which volatility is worth it!

Someone who rides a motorcycle will say that there is less volatility in that vs starting a business.

And that's a fair statement.

Mainly because this person has educated themselves in the field.

What is one person's blind risk is another person's strategic risk.

With learning & executing, a person cannot be **fully** sure of everything.

A person who prepared for their speech can be doing everything right...

However, on speech day, someone pulls the fire alarm when they are about to get to the good part of the talk.

Something like that is capable of happening.

So what should the speaker do?

Move like a coward?

If the speaker is thinking about the chance of someone pulling the fire alarm WHILE they are speaking, then their mind will not be present.

They will sound unsure & weak.

This is the time to unlock strategic faith.

The speaker should prepare.

Then let go of control.

This is equivalent to them turning on the metaphorical light.

'Metaphorical light?'

Yes, faith is like a light switch.

Anything other than ON...is OFF.

A light switch does not generate **any** light if it's toggling in the middle area.

That's because the circuit has not been closed.

Likewise, faith does not generate any bulletproof courage if it's toggling in the middle area.

That's because intention has not been activated.

Strategic faith is like a light switch.

Do all the work in the back end.

Practice for your speech.

Record your talks.

Watch it back.

Whatever is within your control, optimize it to the best of your abilities.

But ultimately, all things have a chance for risk.

When you have done the backend work to the best of your abilities....

Fall back.

Turn the light switch on.

Move with unshakable courage.

That's strategic faith.

FLAWLESS MEMORY

You ever got a question that gave you a compliment in the process?

'Hm... I'm going to need an example.'

A question like:

-Yo, how'd you get so muscular?

This question implies that you are muscular.

A question like that not only inquires something, but also gives a compliment in the process.

This is a charming move, accidental or not.

One of the times I got a question like this was when someone asked:

'Yo, what kind of teleprompter do you use for your YouTube videos?'

Implying that I read off some screen in the back.

I told him I didn't use one.

Then he asked:

'Then how do you remember everything??'

I like a questions like these.

Because it brings awareness to something that I'm proud of.

Which is my memory.

How much does memory weigh?

-Can't weight it.

How tall is memory?
-*Can't measure it.*

How does memory smell?
-*It'll smell like whatever you are recalling at the moment.*

In the modern world, it's easy to run for the notes.
Buy more highlighters.
And get a bunch of gizmos from the external world to 'remember' things.

My question is;
Why not use your internal world?

When I was 8 years old, my elementary school was right by a retirement home.
The students would be taken their every month to volunteer.

I recall my teacher would frame it as a 'field trip.'
Not sure which side of the world you're reading this from...
But a 'field trip' is supposed to be a fun trip that the school takes the students on.

What could possibly be enjoyable about going to a retirement home??

Not only did we go to the home...
But we had to volunteer as well!

Sounds like child labor to me.
Screw you Ms. Shepherd!

But as I would interact with these elderly people, they were often very nice.

They acted like little kids themselves.

I heard that the older someone gets, the more they start acting like they did when they were kids.
And this seemed to be true.

The nurses would try to get the folks in the retirement home to do things they didn't want.
Like eat on time.

The teachers would try to get the students to do things they didn't want.
Like arrive on time.

Therefore, the kids & these elderly folks had something in common:
A Rebellious Attitude.

We would get paired with multiple people each visit.
So during each trip, I'd get to know roughly 4 of the members.
And for next trip, I'd get to know 4 more new members.

One day, I had gone through 3 different people, all elderly men.
The final person I was paired up with was a woman named Susan.

Margaret and I were getting along.
'Wait, you just said her name was Susan!'
That's what she told me...

Then she told me her name was Margaret.
Then she told me her name was Jessica.

It was bizarre because she would remember me for a while.

Then she'd have a split personality & go into another zone.
Then come back.

She'd say:
'Forgive me, my memory isn't what it once was.'

Although you could not see memory, feel it or touch it...
It was impactful.
Once she was losing her memory, she began losing her identity.

I was a little kid at the time, so didn't think much of it.
But nowadays, I cover soft skills from multiple angles with the ArmaniTalks brand.
Therefore, I see why memory is so important.

You can't create something out of nothing.

Some of the most prolific creators you know are data warehouses.
They know a lot.
They remember a lot.

You don't use what you don't cherish.
I don't hate on people who take notes.
I see the need for it.

But sometimes, I wonder how many people who go diving for detailed notes do that because they are **completely unaware** of how powerful their memory is.

It's when we exercise memory that we understand its infinite potential.
If you can remember a grudge with crystal clarity.
Then you can remember information which will serve you....with crystal clarity.

UNFAIR & UNJUST

Whenever a large amount of people get together, volatility is introduced.

That's just how the game goes.

When human egos & initiatives are involved, factor in chaos.

In the beginning of the year, I recall watching this popular podcast that was on top of the world.

There were 4-5 major players who made moves for this podcast.

-2 hosts.

-1 producer.

-And 2 guys that were responsible for bringing on the guests.

As time went by, you can guess what happened.

Things started to fall apart.

One day, one of the hosts opened the show by saying that the 2 people who were responsible for booking the guests were fired.

I didn't hear much of a rebuttal from the 2 fired employees for some time.

Then a few months goes on by.

That's when the 2 fired employees decided to create an expose video breaking down how horrendous that podcast was ran.

They broke down why they were unjustly fired.

From the 2 fired employees, 1 of them **doubled down** on their rage.

He started to go on other shows talking about the unfair treatment he was given.

Show after show, he was 'exposing' these hosts.

Others eventually began making fun of him:

'You got fired bro, move on!' said the general public.

This was a lesson into psychology.

I knew exactly what this guy was going through.

In my undergrad years, I used to be responsible for throwing parties in my organization.

And it made me realize how stressful it was to get people to come to an event.

The constant rejections.

The constant follow ups.

The constant saying one thing & doing another.

On party day, most people assumed that others just 'randomly' came.

Not factoring in my hard work & hours of coordination.

Younger me felt underappreciated.

I'm sure for this fired employee, consistently bringing in guests required a lot of effort.

Follow ups, cold dm'ing, rejections etc.

And I'm sure he believed he played a big role on the podcast's rise.

He probably thought:

'How lit would this show really be if it was just these 2 hosts & no guests??'

However, despite his contributions, he wasn't paid much, if anything at all.

That's why he was going from show to show venting about how he was treated unfairly.

Even though this guy acted like a clown afterwards, showing his emotional weakness....
It goes onto show how people make decisions.

They make decisions to elevate themselves in some way.
There is a desire to increase.
It's natural.

When the desire to increase is not being met, then a person feels bored.

Being bored every now and then is normal.
Being excessively bored is a red flag!
It's a sign of depression to come.

The desire to increase isn't just about money.
It's also about knowledge.
Entertainment.
Food etc.

Each person is different.

When the desire to increase is challenged by someone else, that's when a person FEELS like they were treated unfairly.

That's what happened in this scenario.
The guy who booked the guests probably wanted recognition.

Maybe he was bringing in the guests to show that he was capable of more.
Maybe he wanted to be the 3rd host?...

But getting fired out of nowhere like that hurt his pride.
So he went kamikaze mode...

What he did to get fired was not something he fully disclosed
either.
Therefore, I doubt he is guilt free.

This is why big corporations have so many fallouts.
Even introducing 1 person into a system leads for infinite chaos.

They smile to your face.
Then 3 years later, they are trying to take down everything you
worked for.

That's why it's smart to be aware of the 'desire for increase'
concept.
It's easier to conduct deals that way.

How can I help the person elevate in some way?

A starving guy probably won't care too much for knowledge at the
moment.
He'd probably prefer a sandwich.
At that moment, his desire for increase comes down to food.

Just know this...
A person who is treated unfairly may suck it up for some time.
But assume that most people do not have emotional control.
You never know who can pull a kamikaze.

Life is better when you factor karma into the mix.
What goes around, comes around.
That's a life law.

PATIENT WOLF

You act out the definitions that you assume.
So if you think a socially intelligent person is loud & abrasive,
then that becomes the 'ideal' for charisma.

Eventually, the measurement of success is going to become:
-Who over talks the other person the most.
-Who holds the spotlight the most.
-And who is acting the most 'alpha.'

This is counterproductive.
May lead to short term success.
But overall, it leaves a poor taste in the other person's mouth.

Socially intelligent people are patient wolves.
-Patient to maintain composure.
-Wolf to show activity.

A blend of the 2 prevents a person from acting like a jackass.

Not only are they patient, they can see the invisible.
Remember this:
Intent is invisible.

It's difficult to spot what intent someone is moving with.

John & Mikey may physically be doing the same activity.
-John is doing it for recognition.
-Mikey is doing it to benefit society.
Same move, different intent.

In my new video, I explain how POWERFUL people make friends.

Not powerful in terms of status.

Powerful in terms of spirit.

It's much different than the masses.

These people focus on the invisible & the intent before all else....

CONSEQUENCES

Emotions come and go.
But the consequences can come and stay...

There was a boy throwing a house party when his parents left for a trip.

The house party wasn't supposed to get too big.

But it turned out to be big.

Plenty of the other locals came.

They invited their friends.

And those friends invited their friends.

Network effect.

A party that was supposed to have 30 people ended up having 150+ people.

Attendees were drinking alcohol.

The boy who was throwing the party felt like "the man."

The person who throws the party wields the most power for the night.

There was a party attendee who had too much too drink and was being loud and obnoxious.

The powerful host who was throwing the party told him to pipe down, in an aggressive way.

The loud mouth didn't like how he was spoken to, so he ignored the host.

Being ignored infuriated the host.

He pushed the loud moth.
The loudmouth pushed him back.

Eventually, the 2 were having a scuffle.
What started of as a pushing contest, soon came to blows.

The host asked for help from his other friends.
That's when his friends jumped in and started beating up the loudmouth.

They started hitting the kid hard.
Held his legs down.
Punched him on the ribs.
And kicked him on the head.

Soon, the loudmouth was no longer loud.
He was silent.

Other party attendees looked in shock.
Was he dead?

The host realized what this seemed like.
He put his ears close to the loudmouth & and told the other party attendees:
'Don't worry guys, he is all good!'

Since most of the attendees were tipsy or drunk, they celebrated and went back to minding their own business.

The host & the friends took the loudmouth's body to the car & placed him in the trunk.
Then they drove him to the park.

That's where the host & the friends lit the loudmouth's body on fire.

The host & the friends felt bad for killing the guy.

But the guilt was drowned out by the relief they felt for getting off scotch free.

Until a few weeks passed by.

Officers came to the host's house & cuffed him.

"You have the right to remain silent. Anything you say can and will be used against you in a court of law...."

His parents looked in utter confusion.

This had to be some kind of mistake.

The host looked back at his parents knowing that nothing was ever going to be the same.

The officers took the boy to the interrogation room.

'Don't bother denying the crime. We have witnesses who said what went down in the party. Did you personally know the boy that you burned alive?'

The host looked back in shock:

'Wait, he was alive???'

'Yes, he was,' the office responded.

'Yes, he was...'

The host & the friends involved in the party were sentenced to life in prison.

Not only did the host ruin his life, but the accomplices ruined their lives as well.

The lives of all parties would have been different if the accomplices separated the host & the loudmouth, rather than join the host & jump the loudmouth.

The scenario may have been much more different if the host had a gentle tonality.

The type of tonality that conveys the message without showing disrespect.

Soft skills aren't just about learning how to talk to people.

When perceived with the right lens, soft skills can save your life.

TOUGHENING UP

I wrote a blog recently about dealing with mean comments and cyberbullying.

I took an alternate path to this blog.

Much different.

The traditional advice talks about how to get people to stop cyberbullying others.

Although I think that's a noble intent, I think it is more effective to **toughen up.**

Make the mind so strong that:

Mean comments become just another comment.

This isn't impossible to do.

There is a section in Jimmy Kimmel's show called:

'Celebrities reading mean tweets.'

I rarely watch the Jimmy Kimmel show.

But every now and then, I watch the snippets of the mean tweets section.

I find it hilarious when these celebs read off mean tweets, with a comical musical playing in the background while they laugh at themselves.

Turning darkness into humor builds thick skin like non other.

Recently, I have been reading Will Smiths Memoir which is a great book.

I thought it was going to be an upbeat book which showed how Will Smith was the man.

Instead, I saw the opposite.

Each chapter is divided into an emotion.
Where the beginning chapters are very dark and it progressively gets lighter.

In the beginning of the book, Will Smith talks about his relationship with his father, also known as 'Daddio.'
I'll be calling him 'Daddio' for the rest of this email rather than constantly calling him 'Will's father.'

Will loved his father's intense work ethic & desire to provide for the family.
Where a lot of Will's friends had deadbeat dads, Will's dad always showed up.

Despite the good parts, Daddio also had a dark side.
He was an alcoholic.

When he would get drunk, he would get angry.
He'd often hit Will's mom during moments of anger.

One time when Daddio was hitting Will's mom, she said:
'You can hit me, but you can never hurt me.'

That was a lifechanging moment for Will.
It showed him that perception can **always** be controlled.
No matter how dark the situation is.

Learning to toughen up is probably one of the most crucial skillsets for communication.
Others aren't required to be nice.
There are a lot of people who write mean comments & talk shit because they are bored.

Often, the narrative is:
'How can we get these people to stop??'

But it's much more strategic to say:
'No one can hurt me.'

This is when an invisible shield gets activated within.
And it leads to a state of fearlessness.
That fearlessness leads to supreme creativity.
And that supreme creativity leads to effortless stories, insights, and ideas.

MODERN MAGIC

If we told our ancient ancestors of the kind of technology we have today, they wouldn't believe it.

They'd be like:
'Yea right boy, what you smoking!'

Then we would have to say stuff like:

- *Trust me, there's this thing that allows you to fly.*
- *I'm serious, you can talk from London to Australia without leaving your room.*
- *There are gadgets where you can see people move. It's called a TV.*

They wouldn't believe it.
They would have considered it magic.

Well, technology **is** magic.
It's not the magic with tricks and illusion.
It's the real deal.

But it's hard to be grateful for something when there is a lack of knowledge.
Knowledge is the predecessor to gratitude.

An example is my shirt.
I don't really care how it got designed.
I just want to make sure that it fits and looks good on me.

But for a person who designs shirts for a living, they are like:

'This is a pretty big deal. Allow me to share how **intricate** this is.'

Knowledge allows the mind to perceive intricacies.
And by perceiving intricacies, the mind develops a grateful attitude.

That's why learning how technology works allows the modern magic to be set in motion.
But that's not the magic I'm referring to.

'What could be as magical as technology?'
Writing.

I would say writing is just as magical.
The reason why is because writing allows for:
-Transference of mind.
-Ability to create pictures in other people's minds.
-Influencing behavior at will.

Technology by itself doesn't mean much.
All technology out there was predominantly built for 2 reasons:
1. To help people communicate better.
2. To help distract people from their mind.

Therefore, at the core of **all** technology is a human.
And writing is one of the most effective ways to communicate with a human.

Not any kind of writing.
'Then what kind?'
Simple writing.

I believe this is the future of writing.

Where simplicity takes over.

I hated to read growing up because it felt like I was reading.
If I feel like I'm reading = Poorly written book.
If I feel like I'm not redoing = Properly written book.

The mind should glide through the book.

When the mind glides, that's when the mind focuses on what matters vs what doesn't.

I hated writing in school, because teachers rewarded writers who made their work hard to read.

There was a girl who won an essay writing contest.

She read her essay out loud.

The essay had a scene where a table was being described for 3 minutes.

I found out the table had nothing to do with the plot.

Then why am I hearing it being described for so long?!

It's because that's the writing they want. A lot of flowery language that focuses on the minors.

If the table doesn't move the plot forward, then I don't need to spend so much time making my mind picture it in detail.

A simple word like 'table' is enough for the mind to reproduce it for the narrative's sake.

In 2000s, writing complex showed you were smart.

In 2020s, writing simply shows you are smart.

Technology's rapid progress is speeding up the creative writing revolution as well.

All games are better when there are rules.
At first, the rules seem to take away from creativity.
But overtime, the correct rules seem to ADD onto creativity.

Well, there is a new rule.
Simplify your writing.

See if your writing can be read by a:
-5-year-old.
-Person whose first language isn't English.

When this rule has been added, writing evolves.
Personalities evolve.
And persuasion happens at scale.

If you were to ask me, that sounds like modern magic.

MY FRIEND TRICK

Back in 2000s, there was a clear distinction between a marketer, a salesman, a product developer and much more.

In 2020s, it's not unusual to see all positions bundled into 1 person.

'Why are the categories disappearing?'

I would say it's a hybrid of:

- More information.
- Easier accessibility.

If you wanted to start a business in 2000s, most of it was on physical land.

And to get a piece of the physical land, there were certain rules that needed to be abided by.

- Sign a lease.
- Hire someone from your geographical location.
- Get fliers made.
- Get office supplies.

Etc.

Nowadays, setting up a business is different.

Especially if you are doing it online.

For example: to start a YouTube channel, all you really need is your phone and a google ID.

That's it.

But ease of accessibility is not always a good thing.

It's easy for the older generation to be like:

'Look how easy it is to set up a business nowadays. Back in my days, it was much harder to set up.'

When it's easy to set up a business, that means more people begin doing it.

When more people begin doing it, it leads to potential saturation.

With the ease of accessibility in starting a business nowadays, you are competing against the world....

Which brings me to my next point:

Competition mindset in this era is not too smart.

It's better to cooperate.

A competition-based mindset is smart when the resources are scarce.

Such as physical lands.

But a competition-based mindset is not smart when the resources are abundant.

Such as the internet.

In the internet, it's much smarter to collaborate.

And when collaboration is key, a lot of information needs to be learned.

To know who to collaborate with, it's great if you know a little bit about their field as well.

When you have o idea of the task that you're hiring for, then chances of getting ripped off rises.

'I need to charge you 1500$ dollars to edit your 10-minute podcast,' says the scammer.

Then the scammer proceeds to bring up a bunch of words that you don't know the definition of.

But if you understand some basics of podcast editing, you'll know when you are being taken advantage of.

That's why a lot of entrepreneurs of the modern generation are **polymaths**.
They know a lot about a lot.

Eventually, when their hard work is paying some dividends in profits, they start hiring people.
And this is when collaboration is **tested.**

'What do you mean collaboration is tested?'
A lot of people can go sour.

They start off bright.
Meet deadlines...

But other times, they will be in a bad mood.
Or they have personal problems that cause **you** to miss deadlines.

It's easy to cuss someone out when you don't see their eyes.
A lot of talent nowadays are communicated with virtually.

It's easy to be like:
'I'm going to fire them anyway. Before I do, how about I tell them to fuck off as a going away present?'

But that's not smart.
'Why not?'
Because you never know when you may need someone.

I'll give you an example.

Recently, I've decided to get some of my popular books and convert it to Spanish.

The first one up is **Speak Easy**!
The manuscript translation is complete.
I just need the modified cover.

The guy who did the cover was being very lackadaisical about making the changes.
So, I said he didn't need to make the changes.
Just send me illustrator file and I'll have someone else do it.

This guy couldn't even do that.
It was a simple drag and drop.
But he kept delaying it.

This upset me.

What could have been done in 1 day became a 14-day nightmare.
This is when I hit him with a message that allowed him to soften up.
I said:
'My friend, I would appreciate if you could send me the file.'

When I wrote that, he sent it the next day.

I don't know about his personal problems.
He's normally a very punctual guy.
Despite his bad mood, the 'my friend' allowed him to do the favor quickly.

Once he gave me the file, he shot back with a message of:
'Dear friend, sorry for the delay. Here you are.'

The phrase 'my friend' is very similar to giving someone criticism with a gentle tonality and a smirk on your face.

It's softens the blow.

This strategy allows you to remain composed as well.

In this era with a lot of virtual communication, it's hard to assess tonality.

When you cannot hear someone's tonality, it's hard to understand the level of urgency.

Other times, a harmless message may seem harmful because the message was typed with sharp words.

Words that the other person from a different culture perceived as disrespect.

Bottom line:

- There is **a lot** of room for confusion.

That's when a simple 'my fiend' becomes a virtual body language move that allows you to collaborate rather than annihilate.

It's builds bridges rather than builds walls.

When someone is not meeting deadlines....

Or when a friendship is about to turn sour...

See if you can hit them with a 'my friend.'

That will often allow all parties to win.

NONLINEAR FUNNELS

One of the most popular words in online business has been 'funnel.'

I'm sure you've heard of it.

And it's not only for online business.

It's with interactions in general.

Wide on top, narrow on bottom.

Let's say I want to get a bunch of sand from a bag into a water bottle.

Rather than pouring the sand from the bag straight into the water bottle...

I'll put a funnel in the water bottle.

Then I'll pour the sand into the wide side of the funnel, so it gradually goes into the water bottle.

No mess.

Another example of a funnel is picking up a client.

Let's say you market yourself through:

- Twitter
- A business networking group
- Past clients

Those different mechanisms bring in a lot of leads.

You have the 100 leads fill out a form.

Only 10 fill it out.

And from the 10, you decide to work with 1.

The wide 100 turned into a narrow 1.

'Okay...so what does this have to do with communication?'

I'm here to tell you that funnels are evolving.

Traditional funnels go in 1 direction, and I'm not talking about the boy band.

In our era, funnels go in multi-directions!!

I was surprised to learn this.

If I work with someone on a **service**, I ask them how they found me.

They say something along the lines of:

'Initially, I found you on Twitter. Then I found out you had a YouTube. I saw 8 of your YouTube videos and saw that you had a book out. In the book, I recall you mentioned one of your services. So, here I am.'

I'm thinking...whoa!

That's so unpredictable.

That's when my perception of content changed.

Before, I thought I was just making a 'YouTube video' or a 'podcast.'

Nowadays, I view content as little people scattered around the planet who will answer questions and promote me when I'm taking a nap.

This is a refreshing way to view content creation.

When was the last time you were taken on a nonlinear funnel?

Where you entered from 1 side, then you were taken on a multidirectional journey...until you finally decided to buy?

Tracking down your own nonlinear funnel story will allow you to perceive the strategy behind content creation.

WHY CRITICISM STINGS

There was a period of my life when I was living in Virginia.
I stayed in a big house where a lot of roommates came & went.

While we were getting trained for our roles, we were given free
boarding in this house.
Once we got placed in our roles, we had to move out.

The people who were in the house the longest were the veterans.
There was a a point when I was the veteran of the house.
I had seen people come and go.

When I was a veteran, by coincidence, the new batch of people
coming in were all Nepali's.
One's name was Rohan.
The other's name was Minnie.

Minnie wore glasses and was very soft spoken.
She was smart and had a husband back in Nepal.
The thing I liked about Minnie was that she was a great cook.

One day, I go to the kitchen and Minnie's with the other Nepali
girls making dumplings.
The guys were barbequing.

As I was watched the dumplings being made, I thought it was
cool.
There was a process behind it.

You had to wet the dumpling coating.
Put in the right amount of meat.
Then twist it quickly, otherwise, the meat would fall out.

The girls asked if I wanted to try making one.
I accepted.

I failed the first one.
Tried again.
Failed again...
Damn I didn't put enough meat in!
 There were too many air pockets.

By the 3rd time, I was able to make it correctly.
Then I said:
'Alright ladies, I'm going to let you do your thing.'

Which was code for:
'This shits too hard for me!'

Meanwhile, Rohan was barbequing with the other guys in the house.
He was this short guy with a loud voice.

I knew him as the guy who didn't have a filter.
He'd say **whatever** was on his mind.

There was one time I cooked butter chicken for myself and went to the gym.
I was planning on eating it once I got back.

When I came back and checked the fridge, I noticed my chicken missing!
Rohan said:
'Your chicken was dry. Do better next time.'

His openness was a good thing.
You never questioned his intentions.

By the time the roommates were done with their dishes, we gathered around the table and began eating.

The girls tried the BBQ.
The guys tried the dumplings.

Soon as Rohan tried the dumplings, he yells out:
'This sucks!'

The guys began laughing.
But the girls didn't find it finny.
Especially Minnie.

She began crying.

She was the newest person in the house at that point, so she didn't know about Rohan's openness.
The other girls went to console Minnie.

Rohan looked confused.
He asked:
'What'd I say?'

For Rohan, being blunt was his nature.
It was not personal.

'So why couldn't Minnie see that, Armani?'
It's because criticism stings.

There's a reason it stings.

It stings for the same reason someone hates eye contact.

When I was 16, I hated eye contact.

The reason I hated it so much was because when someone looked me in the eyes, I felt like they were looking at **ALL** of me.

It didn't feel like they were just staring at my face.

It felt like they were getting a 360 view of me.

A few years later, I was at my job.

I got my work done for the day and began surfing the web.

Then I stumbled across a psychology article that broke down why people hated eye contact.

One of the reasons was:

'Because it feels like your whole body is being watched.'

When I saw that, I was like:

'Whoa!! That's literally how I felt as a youngster. So I wasn't crazy. This was a real psychological concept.'

When someone articulated my internal world for me, it felt like a breath of fresh air.

This fuzzy concept now became real.

Well, it's similar with criticism.

Rohan was only criticizing the dumplings.

But to Minnie, it felt like SHE was the one being attacked.

The reason that this happens is because generalizations are a default state and nuances are earned.

If I don't know much about democratic politics.

But the 2 democrats I know are assholes...

Then my generalizing brain will automatically be like:

'All democrats are assholes.'

I need to put in work to get the nuance added in.

I need to acknowledge that my brain will generalize...it's the nature of it.

Then I need to control my emotions to learn about the party that I vehemently disagree with.

That's why emotional intelligence is more important than intellect.

With poor emotional intelligence, a sharp intellect is a liability, not an asset.

More often than not, when a critic is critiquing you...

It will feel like ALL of you is being attacked.

But it's important to keep perspective.

'No, this criticism is just attacking the skill.'

'This criticism is just attacking the dumplings, not me.'

The critic morphs into a hater when they stop critiquing the skill and begin attacking the person.

But that's a talk for another time.

MULTIFACETED

A popular phrase that gets thrown around is:
'Niches get riches.'

I believe this is true to a certain extent.
However, it can lead to a destructive mindset when you're focusing on the bigger picture.

To market a product through a niche is wise.
To market a human through a niche is not wise.

It's much better to think:
'What is my theme?'

By focusing on the theme, it allows you to have a wider view of yourself.
Rather than just being a plumber.
Now you view yourself as the fixer of things.
This allows you to talk about plumbing.
Along with a variety of other topics.

It's easy to think overly narrow.
Especially with content.

I was watching this interview a while back of this famous RnB singer.
The singer seemed pissed in the interview.

He had the reputation as a bad boy and was having trouble finding love.
The interviewers were reinforcing his image as the bad boy.

Eventually, the RnB singer was like:

'Just because I make songs about having sex doesn't mean that's what I'm doing all day!'

I'm sure a lot of people heard this RnB singer's songs and eventually started to put him in a box.

That frozen content is what others perceive him as.

And soon, he may begin perceiving himself as the same thing as well.

My prediction for the future is that people will not be loyal to people.

They will be loyal to universes.

By thinking in themes, 1 man will become a universe by themselves.

They will become a 1-man Disney, Marvel, and Universal Studios.

The future is bright.

Think more of yourself.

You are not only your skill.

You are multifaceted.

REFLECTIONS

Every now and then, there is a tweet that captures my curiosity.
One of the tweets was:
'Name one book that has changed your life.'

The tweet showed up on my feed.
When I saw it, I noticed there were a lot of comments on it.
I went through the tweet.
Maybe I'll find a book that I never heard of.

One of the commenter's on the tweet wrote:
'Meditations by Marcus Aurelius'

One guy asked the commenter:
'What impact did this book have on you?'
The commenter wrote back:
'If I didn't have this book after my divorce, I'm pretty sure I would have killed myself.'

That was a mighty endorsement for the book.
So, I bought it to check it out.

The book was a collection of personal writings by Marcus.
Marcus was a powerful Roman Emperor.

That part didn't intrigue me.
What intrigued me was that he never sat down and was like:
'Let me write a book.'
He was just writing his insights down.
That's when I learned:
One person's reflections are another person's insights.

SHORT FORM CONTENT

There have been plenty of times when I was unable to see something because I only viewed it from my lens.

After some time, I viewed it from someone else's lens and my perspective evolved.

The evolution of perspective wasn't easy.

It took time and happened organically.

One of the first times it happened was with audiobooks.

I used to be in this business networking group where a truck driver was a guest.

He said he drove a lot and rarely **read** books.

He listened to them instead.

He found out I had a book in the market and said he'd listen to it if I made it available on audio.

I thought:

How many people other than this guy really listens to their books?

I found out later on...

A lot.

It was an annoying ad on YouTube that eventually peaked my curiosity.

I went ahead and pulled the trigger.

Text -> Audio

Therefore, my perspective on audiobooks completely changed.

Later, I had a very negative perception of tik tok.
 I'd see weird stuff anytime I opened it.
I made a mental note:
This is something I will never touch.

The main reason I downloaded it in the first place was because one of my clients wanted to record more videos.
And he chose tik tok as his go to platform.

Recently, I had coffee with an entrepreneurial friend.
He was like:
'Bro, you have such a big library on YouTube. You should clip it and post it on tik tok.'

I rolled my eyes when I heard the phrase.
Internally, I was like:
'No man, that app is ridiculous!!'

But he said I should check it out.
I let him talk, but that was about it.

Later, curiosity got the best of me.
I turned a 13-minute clip into a 45 second clip.

Once I looked at it, I was mesmerized.

It's not the followers or the views that motivates me.
It's building the portfolio.
The body of work.

I view content like a realtor views houses.

A realtor wants to build their portfolio.

Get homes in different neighborhoods.

Maybe get some apartments, houses, duplexes etc.

A person who builds content should hopefully expand their empire.

Books, blogs, podcasts, videos and much more.

When I saw short form content, I realized it was a unique angle to pre-existing material.

I got a completely **different perspective** to prior YouTube videos.

There were signs all along too.

I have a podcast where I release a new episode every Tuesday, Thursday, and Saturday.

I don't promote it too much.

It's mainly an experimentation zone for me to articulate my ideas out loud.

Since publishing 400+ episodes, a lot of people organically discovered the podcast.

One of the listeners?

The founding father of the fraternity that I'm in.

How random is that??

He said one of the things he loved about the podcast was how short the episodes were.

He was like:

'I can get through 3 episodes on my way to work!'

He bought up the length.

But it went over my head.

'So, what's the moral of all of this Armani?'
The moral of all of this is often... the answers present themselves randomly.

Something you **never** considered in the beginning stages suddenly becomes a leverage point.

This is why I'm not a big fan of business plans.
I believe business plans will be an archaic concept in the upcoming age.

The only thing that should be in the business plan is a grand vision.
But the plan to get there?
That's moldable.

It's because the world is changing fast.
Being nimble is a form of power.

Therefore, turn down the biases at times.
That's when you may be presented with a perspective that leads to an aha moment.

GLITZ N GLAM

Around 2018 or 2019, I had a call with a guy named Chris Johnson.

As of late, I found out he was blowing up on Instagram.

Back then, his account on Twitter was small.

We were all in the same mastermind.

That's how I was initially introduced to him.

One day, he was going to have a webinar on how he turned his watch company into a 6-figure business.

I thought that was interesting.

I saw some clips but couldn't watch the whole thing.

Later, he released a product on how to make money through Twitter.

He relied only on organic traffic and was able to build a solid business.

I bought the product.

Along with the product, there was a 30-minute consultation that he provided.

So, I took the consultation too.

One day, I got his number and called him.

He was chill.

He gave a lot of tips and I learned a lot from him.

A few weeks later, his Twitter account began blowing up.

He wrote a viral tweet about glitz and glam.

I forgot how the tweet was worded.

But the general gist was how a plumber makes a lot of money despite it not being a prestigious position.

So many people focus on the prestigious positions, that they undermine the blue-collar jobs.

The main focus of his tweet was to not let the glitz and glam fool you.

I thought about that tweet recently as I was looking at the music business.

I have always been a big fan of hip hop growing up.

My brother loved rock music.

And I loved rap and rnb.

I noticed in hip hop, they use the phrases:
Hot and cold.

If an artist is hot, that means they are doing well for themselves.

If they are cold...

Then bye-bye buddy.

Your career is officially over.

I thought that was sad.

There were a lot of artists that I have seen come and go.

They had some attention on them.

But where are they now?

Idk.

Want to know who doesn't have to worry about being hot and cold too much?

'Who?'

The businessmen in the back.

Although you may have 0 clue what they look like, they are making moves that allow them to **transcend** cycles.

This allows them to make the real money.

Prestige or not.

Michael Jackson was one of the rare few artists who had a smart business mind.

Yes, he was great in terms of making music and dancing.

But what else?

He owned the publishing rights to a lot of iconic songs.

This allowed him to get royalties and licensing payments.

He boss'd up.

When you boss up, you aren't over here caring so much about what trend is hot or cold right now.

Instead, you have more control over your destiny.

There are different ways to gain control depending on the industry.

One form of control is knowing a lot.

This is the form of leverage that's great for a 9-5 job.

There are people who work on a floor with a bunch of other people...

But they have 0 clue how those bunch of people relate to them.

Each company has a SharePoint for a reason.

The SharePoint is the centralized database about the company.

If you want to know a lot...

It's not just about knowing your position.

It's also about knowing other people's positions.

If you know other people's positions better than them, then you have a lot of leverage.

A lot of control.

For the ArmaniTalks brand, what I care about the most is this email list.

That's why I give a lot of stuff away free here and do my best to respond back to anyone who emails me.

This list is my main priority.

Because I own it.

It's my own distribution channel.

So, I don't care what's hot or cold right now.

Because this list is what allows me to talk about topics that I am genuinely curious about.

But here's the thing...

This email list is not glitz and glam.

It's like the plumber position.

A behind the scenes force.

But remember what Chris Johnson said.

He said that you don't always need to be glitz and glam to make an impact.

Heck, it's the behind the scenes forces that you need to keep an eye out for.

FIRED

In some countries, they don't fire you.
Instead, they give you clues.

"Based on your recent performance, we believe it's best that you think about finding options elsewhere."

Why do they do that?

It's because when someone gets fired, their future employers look at them with doubt.
Allowing someone to willingly quit is a compassionate way to fire someone.

But for the most part, in the US, it's not like that!
It's the exact opposite.

Sometimes, they will bring you in their office, leave the door open...
And fire you.

Other times, they won't even talk to you.
They will just send you a message.

I saw this YouTube video recently of a girl from Microsoft who got fired.
She was in an important team as well:
-Azure.

Azure is one of the profitable parts of the Microsoft business.
Apparently, she was doing a good job.

Her boss and her had a good relationship.

So, she was **really** shocked when she got fired out of the blue.
That's when her trust in corporations evaporated.

In the talk, she mentioned another fellow.
I forgot his name, so let's call him Timmy.

Timmy was one of the workers who knew EVERYTHING about
the platform.
Timmy was a subject matter expert.

However, he was very rude and volatile to the team.
Despite his negative attitude, he was safe.
He was one of the untouchables.

Another insight the fired girl had was:
Do your best to make yourself irreplaceable.

This video was presented to me at a strange time because I know
someone who got fired from Tesla recently.

Before, he worked in Amazon.
If he could survive in Amazon, then he could survive in Tesla too,
right?
It was looking like that.

But unfortunately, he was let go.

According to him, he was let go because he felt he was
scapegoated.
To make matters worse, he was scapegoated by one of the people
he trusted:
-His manager.

He had an eerily similar experience as the fired girl from Microsoft .

The world has been talking about the FTX collapse recently.
But what has been getting my curiosity has been the Skillshare payment updates.

The new payment structure has gotten a lot of backlash from the teachers on the platform.
Many teachers are noticing a staggering 60 percent pay cut.

Imagine you go from making 10k a month to suddenly making 4k.
A lot of teachers are complaining about how they just quit their job.
Now, they are finding themselves getting a job again.

I make classes on Skillshare too.
However, I was not too affected by this.

One reason why was because of the niche I'm in.
But another reason why was because I never **fully** trusted Skillshare in the first place.

I really like Skillshare.
It's an easy platform to use.
A lot of great teaches to learn from.

So why wouldn't I fully trust them?

Because most of these platforms are for themselves, first.
That is what the girl learned from Microsoft.
That is what the guy learned from Tesla.

The main takeaway from that girl was to make yourself irreplaceable.

My version of doing that is working on this newsletter.

Create a distribution channel that I fully own.

Every video, podcast, class, and book I send out...

- Is to ultimately bring people here.

The reason I think like this is because I have seen plenty of times people being loyal to the wrong things.

When you're loyal to the wrong things, despair ensues.

In many countries, they are kind when letting you go.

They allow you to willingly quit.

But from my experience, I've **seen** people getting fired.

It wasn't malicious.

But it wasn't nice either.

It was strictly business, bud!

One guy was 65 ish.

His name was Nikesh.

Sat right in front of me.

Cool guy.

But a proud guy.

He talked about how he was "safe."

He was serving in the company for 25 years.

Nothing was going to happen to him!

One day, I come to the office and see Nikesh packing his stuff.

His manager was standing by his side, waiting to escort him out and take his badge.

A girl named Debra told me that Nikesh and his whole team was gone.
Replaced by a PowerShell script.

Much love to Nikesh.
But he had this illusion that he was safe.
I believe he put faith in the wrong things.

He put faith in the company.
He put faith in his years in the company.

While in reality, he should have put his faith in the skills.

My last company was very accommodating of horizontal hiring.
So if you got fired, there would be other teams within the company that could pick you up.

But within the past 25 years, Nikesh thought he was bulletproof.
Once he thought that, he stopped learning.
Stopped sharpening his skills.

He was good enough to click a bunch of buttons.
That was about it.

Once he was let go, no other team wanted to scoop him up.

I'll end on a positive note:

- Put faith in the skills.

A lot of people say:

- Either I win or I learn.

But a few people embody it.

THIEF OF JOY

Mr. Beast is a YouTuber who is very well known for his insane work ethic.

In a recent interview, he talked about what his schedule was like.

I saw the clip on Facebook.

I saw him outline his insane workload.

There was one group of people who said:

'Wow, this guy's work ethic is insane!'

But there was another group who said.

'You consider making YouTube videos as work?'

For the latter group, their idea of work mainly stemmed around physical activity.

The idea of creative work was a joke to them.

That's when someone with physical **and** creative work experience contributed to the clip.

This guy used to be a construction worker.

His job required a lot of physical activity.

After some time, he figured the job out.

He realized he couldn't do this role for long.

So he switched to coding.

Took a bunch of classes and worked a few high end projects.

He said with coding, by the time he was done with a typical work day.. he found it difficult to form sentences.

He wanted his brain to be **off**.

That's when he talked about the differences between the 2 roles.

With the physical job, he was exhausted physically, but his mind wasn't that dulled out.
But with coding, he was fine physically, but mentally dulled out.

Comparing jobs is rarely a smart thing to do.
It's hard to know how difficult a job is until you actually do it.

Just know there is no such thing as a free lunch.
Behind anything that looks easy...
There was effort, grit, and consistency, to make it look easy.

BODY OF WORK

One of my favorite quotes of all time is:

"In times of change, learners inherit the earth; while the learned find themselves beautifully equipped to deal with a world that no longer exists."

This quote was by a man named Eric Hoffer.
I Googled who he was.
And he was a moral philosopher.

That's cool.
I'm sure he has a huge body of work.

And here I am...
Compressing his entire life's work into one line.

That's how it works with a lot of people.
Especially when we remember others.

We consume some of their stuff.
Then we boil down their endless:
-Books.
-Essays
-Videos.
-Interviews.

Into 1-4 key ideas that resonated with **OUR** experiences.

This may seem negative.
The ego may be like:

'These ungrateful consumers. Why can't they have a better memory?!'

But I believe this is also a positive.

If people were to realize how one person's life work is another person's quote..

Then perfectionism would forever melt away.

In that state of embracing imperfections, true creativity will be unleashed.

BOSSED UP

When I was a little kid, there was one time I heard my geography teacher say a curse word.

He said:

'Hell.'

There was a family friend named Sami who was a couple of years older than me.

He told me that once I went to high school, teachers would curse more.

And it would be a lot worse than 'hell.'

He was right.

As I started my career, I noticed a lot of managers would curse.

They would drop f bombs.

One particular manager was named Tom.

I never saw Tom face to face.

However, I heard plenty of stories about him.

I used to work in production support.

So, whenever a system would crash, my team was in charge of getting it resolved.

To get it resolved, I had to set up a call known as the bridge call.

This call would gather a lot of the players who were responsible for the system.

The coders.

The people who use the system.

Key clients.
Etc.

The longer the issue took to resolve, the more people we had to involve.
As hours passed on by, one manager after another joined the call.

Eventually, one of the people started to panic:
'If we don't get this resolved soon, then Tom is going to join!'

I thought this person was blowing things out of proportion.
Now way could Tom be that bad!

5 hours passed on by.

A few people on the bridge went for a smoke/food break.
I was the only person from production support on the bridge.

Suddenly, I hear a beep.
I ask:
'Who joined the call?'

I hear:
'This is Tom.'

Ah...
The mythical Tom.
He sounds harmless!

Out of nowhere, he asks:
'What the fuck is taking so long?! Who the fuck are you?'

I was caught off guard.

I said that I was in the production support team.
Then I explained the situation.

He yelled at me some more.
Then he realized he was yelling at the wrong person.
Tom asked for my manager, Paul.

Paul logged back in after his smoke break.
Tom began yelling at Paul...
Dropping every name in the book.

This dude is a managerial director??
He's so unhinged!!

Tom began cursing out one person after another.
I could hear people's voices trembling as Tom peppered them with questions.

After 12 hours of hell, the problem was resolved.
One by one, the exhausted workers logged off the bridge.

In production support, it's up and down.
Sometimes, it's a nightmare.
Other times, it's so calm that you have nothing to do.

A few months go by.
It's chill...

The one day, we have another emergency.

After 3 hours of no resolution, Tom entered the bridge.
This time, he targeted his wrath on a coder.
The coder's name was Eric.

Tom began probing Eric with a bunch of questions.

Tom was gradually raising his voice.

He was about to yell at Eric.

Until....

'Until what, Armani??'

Until Eric yelled at him back.

He yelled at Tom and said:

"If you give me a fucking chance to do my job, I'll update you once I have the resolution!!!'

There was a silence.

No one talked like this to Tom before.

What now?

More silence....

Then Tom said:

'Okay, I'll check back in an hour.'

Whoa, that's insane.

How was Eric able to get away with that?

I soon found out how.

Eric was bossed up.

Meaning that he was in charge of his domain.

He was skilled, had accountability over his application, and was the only one who could get targeted issues resolved.

He was one of the few guys Tom wouldn't disrespect.

I have this inside joke with my friends.
I often say:
'Is that person bossed up or not?'

Being bossed up is not a job profession.
It's an emotional state that is born from competency, accountability, and time.

Being bossed up started off as a joke.
But nowadays, it's a funny way to assess life choices.

I once had this 40-year-old former co-worker hit me up.
He had a YouTube channel that was doing well.
He asked me how to set up a product on Gumroad.

I said I'll show him how.
It's really easy.
Walked him through it step by step.

Afterwards, he says:
'Man, I'm an old dog. I don't get all this technology stuff.'

Then he tries convincing me how I should interview a designer, find a book formatter, and set up his Gumroad profile for him!

All I heard was:
'Do my work for me.'

I said no.
That's not how it works buddy.

I've been shocked to see how many people want stuff done for them.

They have no desire to learn at all.

They want the fish.
But have no desire to learn how a fishing pole works.

Bill Russel was an 11-time basketball champion.
He said something that stuck with me.

He said:
'When you work hard and go the extra mile, that's when you can tell someone to go to hell and not feel bad about it.'

Don't just randomly tell them to go to hell.
But if they try disrespecting you like Tom did to Eric that day, then you can put them in line.

In my book, Eric was bossed up.

CONTROL FREAK

Control freaks often get a bad rep.
But I believe there is logic behind why they behave the way they do.

Sometimes, being too controlling is bad.
Trying to control people rarely works.

Sometimes, being too controlling is not bad.
It leads to creativity.

Why does a control freak's mind work the way it does?
It's because of differences in perspective.

The traditional model of thinking taught in the West is reductionism.
This is when you break down things into its individual components to get a wider array of understanding.

Reductionism is not bad.
However, relying too much on reductionism will make someone lose sight of the bigger picture.

This is when you become the bad kind of experienced.

Where you go into a field.
Learn a niche (specializing).
Go deep into the niche.
And now you are incapable of seeing how the niche relates to the whole.

Creative people are the opposite of a reductionist.

Rather than seeing the individual parts first, they see the full picture first.

Aka: systems thinking.

Once they see the full picture, they find the relevant reductionist concepts to bring the picture to life.

The reason a systems thinker often has control freak like tendencies is because they see the picture **and** the interconnections.

When a reductionist misses a deadline, the reductionist thinks:

'What's the big deal? I just missed a few days.'

But the systems thinker thinks:

'Shit, you missed 3 days. Now the other 2 teams can't begin. This will cause a total delay of 3 weeks after factoring in the interconnections'

Eventually, a lot of systems thinkers will grow out of their controlling tendencies.

They learn to let go...

While other control freaks continue to remain control freaks in a certain domain of life.

And they wouldn't have it any other way...

MOVEMENTS

Recently, there was a pubic figure named Liver King who made an apology video.

He rose to fame because he had a shredded/bulky physique.
He had a primal look.
Walked around shirtless.

I looked at this guy and thought:
'Hm... what's his deal?'

Eventually, he began appearing on a lot of popular shows.
Talking about his philosophy.

His philosophy was to go back to the primal ways.
He talked about eating raw organs, testicles and ... liver.
This message resonated with a lot of people.
They loved the primal philosophy that the Liver King was sharing.

But recently, he came out as being on steroids.
The reason this was a big deal was because he said he never took steroids in a ton of interviews.

In his apology video, he said one of the reasons for his lie was due to self-esteem issues.

I believe the reason is deeper though.
I believe the reason is due to the rise of movements.

I recall the first day I heard of Liver King...
I saw him on the No Jumper podcast.

On the same day, there was another popular YouTuber who made a dramatic video.

It was a video of how the elitists are coming for you.

And to escape the wrath of the elitists, you should join his telegram group.

This YouTuber too was starting a movement.

Looking back at it, I'm like:

'Wait a minute, I witnessed 2 movements in 1 day!'

First of all, what is a movement?

A movement is a **process**.

1. One group feels like they are being discriminated against.
2. The discriminated group is fed up.
3. They coordinate an uprising to change how things work.

I can recall 3 movements off the bat.

First one is the New Atheist movement.

In 2005 ish, I recall a lot of atheists were fed up with the way they were treated.

One atheist said that you could expect to see an alien as a US president before an atheist.

In 2005 ish, the faces of the movement were being appointed.

Richard Dawkins, Sam Harris, Daniel Dennett, and Christopher Hitchens.

They talked about why religion was dangerous for society.

Fast forward more.

The Black Lives Matter movement.

African Americans felt like they were being unfairly treated by the cops.

They wanted change.

The movement formulates.

Another movement was the Me-Too movement.

Many women shared they were harassed in the workplace.

They wanted change.

The movement formulates.

You get the point.

A movement has power when it's happening every now and then.

A movement loses power when it's happening regularly.

'Why do you think there is a rise of movements, Armani?'

I believe it comes down to new media.

On new media (the media created on the internet), there are 2 predominant philosophies for creators.

- Black and white thinking - Mass market appeal.
- Gray thinking – Niched appeal.

Black and white thinking often speaks in generalizations.

They are trying to get as many people to join their message as possible.

Gray thinking is detailed.

Like why water bottles from Australia are more environmentally friendly than Canadian water bottles.

There aren't masses of people searching for a topic like this.

With the gray thinking model, evolution looks like:

Talk about even more highly niched topics. Connect the niched topics. Build creativity. Go deep. Expand.

With the black and white model, evolution looks like:
Start a movement of your own.

Because with the black and white model, eventually, a large group is attracted.
Let's say a million people.

The million people are going to look at the leader and be like:
'Now what?!'

The leader has to think, and they have to think fast.
Because a million people aren't always looking at one person asking what to do next.

That's when a movement begins.
It needs a name and a simple to digest philosophy.

In this case, the Liver King says:
'Now we go back to our primal roots!!'

In the future, I see more and more creators falling into the:
-Black and white model.
-Gray model.

Those who fall into the black and white model will eventually start a movement of their own as they scale.
Eventually, the word 'movement' is going to lose its power.
It's going to be viewed as satire.

'Ah...another movement? It's the 6th one this week!'

Eventually, I see there being a movement on how to start movements.

OBSESSION

Recently, there was news that Gumroad plans to raise their fees to 10 percent.

Which is considered a lot for digital creators.

So, if you're getting paid $10,000 a month.

Now you're giving Gumroad $1,000 of that.

Plus, depending on where you live, there's state tax, federal tax, payment processor fees etc.

This caused an UPROAR.

Many popular creators publicly called out Gumroad and their CEO.

There were also companies siezing their moment.

They were like:

'Come to our platform instead! We only charge a 2% fee.'

This is was a spectacle to watch.

A few weeks back, I talked about the Skillshare pricing change.

A lot of teachers went from making $10,000 per month to $4,000.

As I looked at these 2 different platforms, I noticed the same pattern.

A platform *abruptly* makes a change that infuriates its creators.

Platforms have their own set of stressors.

They have stakeholders to answer to.

Which is why I haven't yet said:

'Fuck Shillshare and Gumroad!'

Because I have no clue who they answer to.
I doubt they woke up one morning and said:
'Let's just screw our creators over.'

Nevertheless, this was a big gaffe on Gumroad's part and can potentially ruin the company.

'What are your predictions for the future, Armani?'
Good question.
It's a bold response, you really want to hear it?
'Yea...'

With the volatility of platforms, creators need to build their own universe.

There are going to be 2 groups of people:
-Those who are obsessed.
-And those who are not.

It's impossible to build a universe if you are not obsessed.

'How does one build a universe?'
It comes down to 2 things:

- Create content.
- Connect content.

These 2 steps repeated over and over eventually leads to the emergence of a universe.

Once the content is created and connected, a person stops relying on 1 platform.

They stop saying:

'I'm a Gumroad creator!'
'I'm a YouTuber!'
'I'm a Tik Toker!'
As if it's some badge of honor.

Instead, these people have a portfolio of variety.
A universe **needs** variety.
Look at our own universe, and you'll see variety everywhere.

Eventually, when breaking news like a platform raising their fees from 3% to 10% happens...
The rulers of the universe will be affected, yes.
But it's nothing that causes them to lose sleep.

It's like one solar system among galaxies of galaxies of galaxies of galaxies of galaxies took a hit.
(Another example is that there is 1 typo in a 4,000 paged book).
Marginal.

While the solar system recovers, the other galaxies will hold the universe up.

This is not a new idea by the way.
-Vince McMahon was obsessed with WWE.
-Sam Walton was obsessed with Walmart.
-Walt Disney was obsessed with Disney.

But the stakes for being obsessed is only going to rise in the next 15 years.
With the ease of access to information technology, the marketplace is global.
More players than ever.

Competition is so high that the competition mindset has become archaic.

It's the creation mindset that dominates.

Building a universe takes time.

It takes grit.

It requires patience and strategic execution.

But with the volatility of platforms, my prediction is that the universe business model will be the best option.

It will be the strategy to weed out:

-Spotty thinkers from long term thinkers.

-Part time players from the obsessed ones.

People hate on obsession..

But when understood correctly, obsession is focus's older brother.

ELIMINATION

-A big part of discipline is doing something.

-Another part of discipline is not doing something.

The second line will determine whether you stay consistent or quit.

Whenever we discover new information that can impact our life, we **feel** good.

Imagine someone introduces you to the gym for the first time.

That's when you go to the gym and begin working out.

You feel good.

Your bodybuilding friend says:

'3 times a week should do the trick for your lifestyle.'

But you are like:

'3 times a week?? More like 3 times a day for me! I have sooo much energy.'

Soon, you become obsessed.

You go in the morning, evening, and night.

You're not a fulltime bodybuilder either.

Still have other priorities and jobs to do.

Can you be consistent?

Even when the motivation fades?

In the beginning, failing and learning the hard way that 3 times a day is overkill is necessary.

This is when you are like:

'Hm... this 3 day a thing is cool and all. But I don't know if I can do it for 10 years. How can I alter?'

Once you find an alternate route, that's when you have more confidence with your decision.

I used to hate that Toastmasters had a timer position.
'Why have a timer?? I can talk for 20 minutes if you would let me!'

Just because I can talk for 20 minutes doesn't mean that I should.
6 minutes will do the trick.

By shaving away the dead ends, now the mind begins to think in **decade by decade increments**.
When it commits to a task, it truly commits.

It understands:
'Yes, I'm in it for the long run. Because I know how to say yes. But more importantly, I know how to say no...'

SELL OUT?

I recently stumbled upon this video that captured by curiosity.
It was by a guy named Jidion.
It was titled:
 "I Sold Out..."

I never heard of this guy before.
But I clicked it anyways.

In the initial stages, I thought it was a joking type of video.
As the video progressed, it got real.
He began hysterically crying.

Apparently he got famous out of nowhere and had too much spotlight on him.
When he had a lot of spotlight on him, it made him lose touch with his roots.
He began to work with popular influencers and popular brands.

One of the popular brands was the NFL.
The NFL asked him to a do a skit for them.
Jidion did the skit.

Then the NFL came back with changes to make.
-*"You need to make it more family friendly."*
-*"Improve your energy."*
-*"Tone it down!"*

After getting all that feedback, Jidion was like:
'Yo, what am I doing?'

That's when he realized he was behaving in a different way than he was used to.

In the beginning stages, it was all about creating art and making good content.

Now, it seemed like he was trying to fit a role.

It's difficult to tell how anyone will behave with a lot of spotlight on them.

I was always amazed how easily great companies could destroy themselves.

As an outsider, I was like:

'How could they possibly make such a big mistake? If I was running the show, I wouldn't have made a mistake like that!'

But I am not the company.

I am an outsider.

It's difficult to tell what quick fame will do to someone.

The whole concept of fame (as we know it) is rather new.

Originally, fame was done through gossiping.

The village would talk bad about you if you did something bad.

The village would talk you up if you had a skill.

'You hear Johannes can fight?'

This type of fame relied on geographical location.

Village, household, towns.

Later, mass communication was introduced.

Radios, telegraphs, TVs etc.

Now, location did not matter.

Later on, the internet was introduced.

The mass communication tools of the 60s were no longer consolidated to a few higher ups.

Now **everyone** had the tools.

Suddenly, people were getting famous quicker than ever!

Even people with minimal life experience.

Throughout the past few years, I've seen a lot of these YouTubers have a mental breakdown for the world to see.

One of the most recent examples was Conor Murphy.

However, this Jidion guy had the awareness to acknowledge he sold out by his standards.

He ended the video on a positive light.

He made the note that he was going to focus on the basics again.

He was going to double down on what he did in the early parts of his YouTube career.

In some ways, straying from your path can be a good thing.

Because once you return to your path, you have the **conviction** that you'll never let the same mistake happen again....

GEORGE LUCAS

I sort of watched Star Wars, but not really.

I saw some movies out of order, but never saw it from the beginning.

Despite never watching Star Wars, I am a fan of the way that George Lucas (the creator of the series) thinks.

His view of storytelling is very **practical**.

He has a Birdseye view of the field.

His view is that you should know a lot about a lot of subjects.

The more you know, the more you can connect a variety of subjects to produce something unique.

Even though his movies have a lot of special effects...

He never lost sight of the fact that the technology serves the story, not the other way around.

George noticed a drawback of being a pioneer.

'What was that, Armani?

Plenty of people lost sight of the big picture of storytelling.

Once George made Star Wars a hit, different studios were like:

'Yes, we need to make a film like that.'

Studios hired different filmmakers and unleashed copycats to recreate a similar film.

These studio heads believed that the special effects was the reason Star Wars was a hit.

However, those copycat movies fell flat.

'Why?'

Because those movies were leading with the technology first, not the story.

When asked what Star Wars was REALLY about, George said: *'It was about politics, psychology, and human nature.'*

That's why the audience resonated with the film.

The special effects simply served as an amplifier.

Those copy cats who were trying to mimic him didn't understand that.

They saw the surface level but missed the **heart** of the film.

One of the toughest things for George was selling the Star Wars series to Disney.

It's because Disney cared more about delivering a hit rather than making a great tale.

He **hated** the Star Wars remake that Disney created.

He felt it lacked depth and moxy.

When you do too much market research, that's when creativity plummets.

Creativity is born through failure and risk.

Disney saw what worked in the past with Star Wars and decided to go the safe route.

^ This was George's opinion at least, I didn't watch it.

It was like his past was making a return to the present.

The same copycats who were mimicking him back in the days were now the same copycats who had the rights to the series.

The main thing I learned from George was to focus on the story and make that the king.

When you lead with the tale, you don't look at the end goal of making a hit first.

Rather, you focus on the plot, the subtle messages, the unique characters etc.

By doing that, the hit is a possible reward.

But it must never be confused as the goal...

CREDENTIALS

There was a day when I was invited to go to a dinner party by the head of the MSA.

This was known as the Muslim Students Association.

I wasn't in the club nor did I want to join it.

The members seemed too cliquey.

But the president wanted to collaborate with an organization that I was in.

He insisted I go to his dinner party.

I said, *okay I'll be there.*

He said something along the lines of:

'*Don't worry, my house is right around the corner.*'

The house took me 40 minutes to get to.

Man, what kind of corner is this?

It took so long!

Once I entered the party, I didn't know anyone.

Now I was second guessing why I even accepted the invite in the first place.

I was hoping the food was going to be good.

The president, Ibrahim, came to me and was like:

'*Hey, you made it! Allow me to introduce you to some people.*'

He introduced me to this guy named Omar who was talking to another guy named Haseeb.

Omar seemed sad.

I began talking to him.

This Omar guy got comfortable me with me really quick.

He was like:

'I was just telling Haseeb that my dad can't get a job. He's qualified too!'

I asked what his dad's qualifications were like.

Omar listed off a bunch of stuff.

Then he said:

'He also has a PhD.'

When he said his dad had a PhD and still couldn't get a job, I was like:

'What?? But he's so qualified!'

Omar said:

*'Exactly. He's **too** qualified. He's losing out on jobs to bachelors and masters degree holders. The companies in his industry don't have the budget for PhD holders.'*

A younger me couldn't even fathom something like that.

I was getting my bachelors at the time.

During that span, I could have definitely seen myself getting a masters and a PhD down the line.

Now there was this guy telling me that his dad couldn't get a job **because** of his PhD?

Clown world!

Later that year, there was this website that was released which shared how much our college professors made.

For some reason, the students thought college professors were broke.

But when we saw the list, we were mind blown!

We saw professors making up to 175,000 dollars plus.
This is in Florida.
Which is a lot.

The teachers weren't aware that the students knew their salary.

We had a cool professor.
His name was Dr. Wiley.
We talked to him like he was one of the boys.

One day, Dr. Wiley was complaining about something.
And one of the kids was like:
'Dr. Wiley, you're making $175,750 plus $6,750 in bonuses. Why are you complaining??'

Dr. Wiley turned around looking shook:
'How the hell do you know how much I make?'

I'm laughing as I'm writing this.
His PhD proved well worth it.

No matter which field it is, there is a good side and a dark side.

Sometimes, being too qualified is not a good thing.
Sometimes, being too qualified allows you to be brave when others are fearful.

Credentials are a subjective topic.
In some industries, they are very important.
And in some industries, they do not matter at all.

PICKY EATERS

To me, being a picky eater does not only mean someone who is picky with food.
It represents someone who is not crafty.

One way that I measure picky eaters is by asking the question:
Are they a pain in the ass to show around?

A while back, I knew a picky eater.
He was someone who would always get fancy with it.

A lot of college kids didn't have that much funds.
Food was food.

But this guy, let's call him Arnie, always had to get cute with it.

When the other kids were down for a quick meal at Taco Bell...
Arnie wanted to pay 20 bucks to sit down and eat somewhere.

I'm all for a great cuisine.
However, that's not where Arnie stopped.
He had this snobby vibe to him.

One day, a bunch of the friends went from Tampa to Gainesville for a tailgate.
We knew this guy at Gainesville who was going to let our group of 5 stay with him.

He was a college kid too.
So, he didn't have that much money.
However, he was doing the best he could.

He bought a bunch of hamburger patties.
But unfortunately, ran out of money for the buns...

The friends were like:
'Bro, you're all good. Thanks for getting the patties!'

By the time Arnie gets out of his 45-minute long shower, he is notified about the eating plans.
In a horrified voice, he was like:
'We are supposed to eat burgers without the buns?! Just the patties?'

This was an unfathomable concept to him.

It's one thing if he asked once.
But he kept bringing it up.
Ruining the vibe.

For the rest of us, it was not a big deal at all.
But for the picky eater, Arnie, it was a massive deal.

Not only that.
Afterwards, we were all going to get blankets and sleep on the ground.
This was a place to rest up until we went to the tailgate tomorrow.

Once again, Arnie acted like a baby:
'No futons or air mattresses?'

He slept on the floor like a wuss.
Making all these whiney noises.

He was soft.
Not a tough guy by any means.

I'm not saying that a person should just eat garbage to prove they are not a picky eater.
But during times of uncertainty, are you capable of adjusting?
And it's not just about adjusting....

But adjusting with your enthusiasm intact.

There is a hurricane headed towards Florida.
And a bunch of people are panicking and stocking up...

I go to Walmart today for some last-minute items.
Most of the food items are gone.
It was like the Coronavirus time when you were lucky to get food.

Chances are that the name brands you prefer are **gone**.
Are you capable of adjusting?
Or are you going to be a baby about it?

Fine dining is a luxury.
Never confuse it as an essential.
When times are tough, you should be able to adjust without a complaint in sight.

NUANCES

Nuances are normally a good thing.
But in the information age, it's often seen as an insult.

When someone says:
'There are nuances to this.'

The opposition is like:
'Oh great. We got a gray thinker. This is a person who lacks conviction.'

Every now and then, black and white thinking is needed.
^But even this line is very subjective.
Very nuanced...
Very gray...

I knew this one kid whose brother got caught in a sting operation.
Let's call the kid Sam.
And his brother's name is Derek.

Derek was 24 years old during the incident.
He was chatting with a girl who he thought was a 12-year-old.
And he drove all the way to Orlando from Tampa to meet up with the 12-year-old.

By the time he went to Orlando, Derek was greeted by the FBI.
Not the local cops.

If it were the local cops, he would have gotten away with a lighter sentence.
But since he was caught by the FBI, he was sentenced to 12 years in prison!!

Sam was shocked.
He couldn't believe that his best friend was going to be gone for so long.

Sam was even more shocked that Derek would be caught in such a heinous situation.

Soon, Sam began doing research.
He wanted to know **why** his brother did what he did.

His studies led him to the conclusion that early concussions increases the likelihood of pedophilia.
Both Sam and Derek were football players growing up.

Apparently, Derek got hit on the head a lot.
And one time, he began spazzing and frothing at the mouth.

Sam began to share this theory around his friends.
Me included.

I had a very black and white approach to this.
I was like:
'Alright bro, I don't know about that...'

My brain shut off the idea.
I tried to be as respectful as possible.
Others were not as respectful.

They cut Sam off.
He was no longer invited to events.

Others even said:
'If Sam could find info like that to justify his brother, he probably knew something was going on.'

Sam insisting something concussion related led to the crime may have been true from his paradigm.

He searched for more information that I never bothered too.

This is where the topic of nuance comes in.

One person's black and white is another person's gray.

The brain doesn't like gray too much.

It because gray is not crystal clear.

The brain likes crystal clear *a lot*.

That's where it gets fulfilment.

But even though the brain doesn't like gray too much, the heart likes it *a lot*.

Because we are gray on something that we know a lot about.

And for us to know a lot, we must care a lot.

Let's say everyone hates Susie's brother, Tommy.

Tommy is brash, rude, and snake like.

But Susie still loves her brother because she has a gray perception of him.

She grew up with the guy.

Therefore, she knows him well and his volatile moods.

I've learned that being too gray is not always a good thing.

Then it's easy for the mind to fall of anything.

Values create value.

Values create value because it creates a filtration system.

Imagine if a great political commentator began doing reviews of toys on his YouTube channel.

Toy reviews are hot right now.

Could he do it?
Yea, he could do it.
However, toys do not pass his filtration system.

Deciding what your values are is a personal process.
The values can come from holy texts.
Scientific texts.
Personal experiences.
All of the above.

The filtration system allows us to determine what is black and white.
What is gray.
And what's black and white for now but may turn gray in the future...

SEASONS

Have you ever seen that person who seemed to have it all?
But worked like it was day 1?

On the contrary, there was someone who was lazy and their life was in shambles.
But still, no hunger.

Why the difference?
Why does the winner continue to work hard?

There has been a lot of talk regarding the law of attraction.
It seemed to be at a fever pitch in 2017.

You think and believe something, then relevant opportunities will come your way.
Act as well.
Don't just visualize and call it a day.

Another remix to the law of attraction is:

- Relevant knowledge is presented.

When you ask a question **with curiosity**, randomly... content will be suggested to you that answers the question.

One of your acquaintances may message you out of the blue with a comment and you're like:
'What the hell?! I was just thinking about this topic recently.'

Has that ever happened to you?
It has happened to me.

I was thinking:

- Why do a lot of winners still work like it's day 1?

Then randomly, I was presented a Vanilla Ice Documentary.

I've heard of him before, but didn't know him that well.
I saw some of his appearances on reality TV.
But couldn't fathom how big he was in the beginning of the 90s.

The documentary laid out how he was multitalented.
He could beat box, rap, and dance.

He had a hit called:
Ice, ice baby.

This song catapulted him to the mainstream.
He was getting worldwide fame and accolades.

Soon, he was on top of the world.
Being invited to all the cool talk shows.
Getting endorsement deals.
Finalizing movies.

Everything he touched turned into gold.

But you know what they say...
With more attention comes more scrutiny.

Others began to get annoyed with Vanilla Ice.
Rap purists said that Vanilla Ice presented a watered-down version of hip hop to the masses.

Reporters who were looking for a story wanted to see who Vanilla Ice *really* was.

Was he who he claimed to be?

Soon, there were reports coming out stating that Vanilla Ice lied about his past.

Back then, the record companies had a lot of power.

The company would create an origin story for their artist so the talent would be better recieved by the masses.

A lot of the origin stories were fabricated.

How much of Vanilla Ice's past distortions were due to malicious intent?

And how much of it was due to the nature of the record business?

Didn't matter.

Vanilla Ice's reputation was destroyed.

Soon, others began making fun of him on late night talks shows.

Business partners stopped returning his calls.

The masses began to question his body of work.

He fell into depression.

Began doing heavy drugs.

And even attempted to kill himself.

Due to a miracle, he survived.

Once he survived, he realized the past was the past.

He was given another chance to reinvent himself.

Nowadays, Vanilla Ice is a different person.

He still gets royalties from his hits in the 90s.

And he invests that money into his new passion:

Flipping homes.

'From a rap superstar to flipping homes??'
Yep.

Vanilla talks about flipping homes like a craftsman.
I believe he had a show about it too.

Point being, Vanilla leaned that life comes in **seasons**.
Early 90s, he was hot.
Late 90s, he was cold.
Nowadays, he seems to be climbing his way to the top.

My question was answered.

The reason that ambitious people always have movement is because they too had a rock bottom moment.
They went from hot to cold.
They didn't know how long the cold would last.

Days
Weeks.
Months...
Years...
Forever??

They thought:
'Damn, if I get another opportunity, then I will never take the hot moments for granted.'

Soon, they became hot again.
But this time, they became hot with **perspective**.

The perspective of:

-Cold times are around the corner.

-I must never rest on my laurels.

-Yes, I'll be grateful for the past.

-But I need to reinvent myself for the future.

Those are the seasons of life.

SIDE KICK

The Amazon affiliate program is pretty unique.

If you get a sale from your link, then all other products that the customer buys... you also get a percentage of.

So, let's imagine you have a blog on tumblers.

And you create a blog called:

'10 top tumblers.'

Jim reads your blog.

He sees 1 tumbler he likes.

He clicks on your affiliate link.

He adds that tumbler to his Amazon cart.

Then he thinks:

'Hm... I should also buy some toothpaste while I'm here.'

So, Jim buys toothpaste.

From there, you get a percentage of the sale for the tumbler **and** toothpaste.

I did a YouTube video a while back that broke down the #1 Storytelling book out there.

It was me recommending Carmine Gallo's, the Storyteller's Secret, book.

That video still gets traffic to this day.

Every now and then, someone enters the link...

They buy the storytelling book...

Then they buy other things too.

I've seen some strange things!!

Sex books.
Hangers.
Kids posters.
Toasters.
and much more.

That YouTube video has generated a lot of revenue.

What's funny about that video is that I'm not selling any of my products.
Instead, I'm being a **sidekick** to a bunch of other products.

Being a sidekick is often seen as an insult.
But nowadays, I see sidekicks becoming cool.

Just because you are a sidekick in one side of your life doesn't mean you are a sidekick in other facets.

Sometimes, a certain act just means a lot more to someone else.
So, if you are in the act as well, then it will be smart to ask:
What can I do to make your life easier?'

By doing that, they will give you some tasks where you are like:
'That's it?'

The tasks you are assigned is way better than the tasks you would have been assigned if you were trying to compete on being the star.

These opportunities are all around.

Anyways, I've been using the word *sidekick* this whole time.
But instead, view it as an *amplifier*.

In electrical engineering, we have a component called the amplifier.

It gets a pre-existing voltage and amps it up.

This allows us to buy a power source for cheap.

And just step it up a bit more with the amplifier to make the entire circuit function.

If you find yourself being the sidekick...

Don't view it as a negative thing.

Instead, view it as being an amplifier.

Without you, the circuit wouldn't function!

FUTURISTIC

A few days ago, I got a message from someone who follows me on one of my platforms.

He was like:

'Hey, I noticed you've been creating shorts. I have a new app that I believe will help you.'

I tried out the app.

I uploaded one of my videos.

It began buffering.

I was expecting that it was going to be one of those apps that let me edit the content and put subtitles in.

But no...

It was more futuristic.

Instead, it was an app that had artificial intelligence go through the video, take parts it deemed relevant, and created a theme behind it.

I uploaded a content piece from my class on editing.

And it the spit out a video on the beauty of overwriting.

That's when I thought:

'How did it know which point to choose?'

It chose a very good point that I would have chosen too.

The app is still in the rudimentary phases.

But I thought:

'Wow, what potential!!'

Imagine if a creator is just responsible for creating a video.
Then the video is upload to the app later.
Then the app chooses the parts it deems important and creates the short.

Time is saved.
Money is saved.

I still don't know how the algorithm choose the points.
Nor did it matter to me.
It just showed me how much potential is out there.

Many people are waiting for the future.
They think it's going to show up one day.
Not realizing that we are living in the future now....

Imagine a guy who was sentenced to prison in 2004 is released today.
The world of 2004 is way different than 2022.

He's going to be like:
*'When **exactly** did the change happen?'*

And you'll be like:
'There wasn't an exact moment, bro. It was just a series of changes that led us here.'

When you think in series, it allows you to experiment and try new things **now**.
Rather than waiting for this ambiguous future to arrive with dread on your face.

Realize there are many people who are perfectly aware that we are living in a futuristic society already.

No reason to be so doom and gloom.

Instead, use this time to create, propose innovative solutions in your industry, and flex your imagination.

The resources are abundant.

But the desire is scarce.

JUSTICE

I never understood Monopoly.
Although I'm sure that Monopoly would be a fun game to learn.

The one thing I know about Monopoly is that there is a place called Park Place and Boardwalk.

The reason that sticks out is because I lived in both those neighborhoods growing up
Park Place second.
Boardwalk first.

When I was in Boardwalk, I would play outside a lot.
My brother and I would play with these 2 other kids:
-Uchash and Deep.

Uchash and Deep were younger than my brother and me.
I took Uchash under my wing.
My brother took Deep under his wing.

We did what any kids would do.
We'd play hide n seek.
We'd play sports.
And we'd race.

We'd race a lot.

I was getting annoyed because Deep would always beat Uchash.
Uchash was taller though.

I'd think:

'You have long legs fool! You should be beating this short weasel!'

But no.
Deep won over and over again.

One day, I had an idea.
I was going to have them race.
And I was going to be the referee.

I was going to be one of those running referee's.
Ready, set, GO!!!

As usual, Deep was poised to win.

But last minute, I ran in front of Deep to slow him down.
I gave the illusion that I was rushing to the finish line to see who was going to win.

That's when Uchash caught up and overtook Deep.
Uchash finally won!!

Before I could celebrate, there was a woman marching towards me.
It was Deep's mom.

'You ran in front of my boy! That's why Uchash won. Have them race again!'

This lady was yelling at me.

I must have felt brave because I argued back with her.
I believe I was 7 years old at the time.
I said:

'No, your son lost. Uchash won!'

Uchash nodded his head with bravado.

The mom walked away enraged.
She didn't talk to me for a couple of days.
Before, she used to come outside while the kids were playing.

The race scandal really pissed her off.

Back then, I thought she was blowing things out of proportion.
Nowadays, I see her anger was justified.

I did something unfair.
To make matters worse, my unfair act was targeted towards her son.

Looking back at that moment, I realize I did another thing wrong.
'What's that?'
I gave Uchash the illusion that he won.

There were a lot more lessons from that moment.
But one of the biggest lessons is that humans lash out when they believe they have been treated unfairly.

A lot of controversies happen because people forget this **core human nature** principle.

A principle has utility when it has versatility.
Understanding the unfair principle is a way to reduce speech anxiety.

'Speech anxiety, forreal?'
Yes.

Because with speech anxiety, it's all about me, me, me.
That mentality makes us ego centered.

Switch perspectives for a second.
Walk a mile in someone else's shoes.
Zzz....

Most people don't have fun lives.
No offense.

Their day is broken down into:
Work.
Pay bills.
Watch a show at the end of the night.
Repeat.

To make matters worse, they have created an enemy in their mind, like Deep's mom created of me.
Some enemies deserve to be there, while others are unjustly given that label.

Maybe the enemy is their:
-Parents.
-Boss.
-Failed venture.
-The person who cut them off in traffic etc.

Simply understanding the principle that humans *hate* for things to be unfair...
Gives you a level of clarity.

The clarity wipes away fear as the speaker.

You have control.

Just **1 joke** is all it takes to get the audience out of the turmoil
they have created for themselves.

As the speaker, it's hard to feel anxiety when you're doing
someone else a favor.

This law of unfairness if very big.

I wonder if there is a name for it.

If not, I'll just name it:

'Deep really won.'

DISRUPTION

*A disruption is an innovation that leads to a **radical** change of how things used to operate.*

When was the last time you witnessed a disruption?
There have been plenty as of late.

One example of disruption is Uber.
I recall there was a time when Ubers were not a thing.
We had to rely on a taxi if we didn't have a car.
Depending on your geographic location, good luck finding a taxi.

Christopher got drunk at a club.
He was like:
*'What now? I don't want to call anyone because they will see how drunk I am. Now that I think about it... I'm not **that** drunk.'*

Christopher got behind the wheel.
Then he proceeded to find out he was **that** drunk.
Killing himself and another family in the process.

I'm sure Uber has saved a lot of lives.
Uber caused a disruption.

For a while, this disruption was not met with open arms.
When I was living Jersey, one night, I took a taxi.

The taxi driver said that he didn't like Uber drivers.
The taxi game works differently from the Uber game.

A typical Uber driver has the mentality of:
'I'll pick up Uber on the side.'
They are doing it as a side hustle.

While taxi drivers often view their driving as a career.
They aim to get health insurance and all of that.

The taxi driver was like:
'I don't like these new Uber drivers. Whenever a Uber driver comes to my block, me and the other taxi drivers chase them away.'

Your block?
Man, you sound like a gangbanger!

The Uber disruption had a lot of benefits.
However, disruption comes with **a lot** of animosity as well.

A disruption is rarely accepted with open arms.
There are taxi drivers (members of the previous model) looking at you sideways.

Nowadays, one of the disruptions I see is the low code movement.
Where you don't really need to know how to code to make functionable applications.
It's more plug and play.

Some coders have this dogma to them.
They get so caught up in the coding that they scoff at the low code movement.
'Ah, low code? No, I don't need that. I actually know how to code.'

That was the same attitude that IBM had towards the personal computer.

'Ah, a personal computer? Nah...we actually have infrastructure.'

They viewed personal computers as a toy for hobbyists.
Nothing more.

Same thing happens with traditional publishing vs self-publishing.
'Ah, self-published? Guess you couldn't make it to the big leagues...huh?'

This snobby attitude is what makes people blind to disruption.

The world is in a constant state of flux.
Thinking everything is going to be the same is an illusion.

Even if changes seem slow....
When changes are accepted as the norm, it feels like it happened SUDDENLY.

PRIVILEGE

I used to have a very binary view of privilege.
I thought some people had it and some people didn't.

But after writing on this newsletter for a while, I realized that words are arbitrary.
Who defines the constraints of privilege?

As I wrote on this newsletter some more, I made a shocking realization:
Everyone has some form of privilege.

In mainstream consciousness, the 2 buzzwords are:
-Pretty privilege
-White privilege

Another type of privilege not often talked about is:
-The privilege of having all sense organs working effectively.
Some people are born with one crucial organ not working effectively, aka: Blindness.

What gets talked about a lot are the good sides of privilege.
But what doesn't get talked about enough are the dark sides of privilege.

For example, the wealthy kid.
Jacob was his name.
His parents had connections to the political scene and the schools.

Jacob was set up for life.
Didn't have to work for much.

He cheated thru school.
Was set up for jobs after graduation.

However, as Jacob was hitting his mid-30s.
He was feeling off.

He never created anything for himself.
Instead, it was just given to him.

When he walks in a room, others address him as his dad's son.
'Ronald's kid, right?'

This effects his self-esteem.

When he vents to others, they are like:
'What are you whining about? You had everything delivered to you! There are people who would kill to be in your position.'

Jacob's stuck in the conundrum of:

- Being upset for not creating anything meaningful in his life.

and

- Not feeling grateful for all he has.

Suddenly, a spiral happens.
He begins to act out.

A lot of silver spoon kids royally self-sabotage themselves.
It's a stunning pattern that I've noticed.

'Any idea why this happens?'

My theory is:
When you skip the process, the process finds you.

Another form of privilege is pretty privilege.
A while back, there was this reddit thread that went viral.

It was an AMA (ask me anything) from this very attractive girl
who chose to remain anonymous.
Others began firing off questions at her.

'What's it like to be that pretty?'

'You must get everything handed to you, right?'

'You probably don't have to do any work.'

I was expecting very bubbly responses.
Instead, I saw very dark responses.

'I have to consistently craft polite no's to turn down strangers.'

'By default, others assume I'm an idiot.'

'I'm terrified of losing my looks.'

I'm like, what?
Damn, I thought this privilege thing only comes with the good.
No bad.

But nothing in life only comes with the good.

What the media does is they cherry pick a few people's privileges.
Highlight it.

And remove all low lights.

With all that being said, my view is that if you have a privilege, own it.

If you had wealthy parents who worked hard to make sure that you are set up...

Then get the resources they gave you and *multiply* it.

When the mind has little problems, it starts to feel guilty.

It takes on guilt of our past ancestors.

Our past actions.

And other people's actions.

This is false improvement.

This person who is taking on all this guilt is like:

'See? I'm such a stand-up person. Others should feel guilty like me! That's progress.'

But this is an illusion.

The guilt accepting person isn't **producing** anything.

Some people get ideas easily.

Some people have more connections due to their family.

Some people have genetic gifts that give them a baseline level of athleticism.

And some people have good health.

All privileges to someone else.

Rather than whining about it.

Double down on it and use it ethically,

BOOK COVERS

Within this year, I released a book a month.
Whether it was a short stories book.
A beginner's book on learning a skill.
Or a novel.

My process goes like this:

- Write the manuscript.
- Edit the manuscript.
- Proofread the manuscript.
- Then get the manuscript formatted (so it goes from a Word document to fitting in a paperback/Kindle).

As it's getting formatted, I'm making the cover.
I don't have Photoshop, so I work with a designer.

I can't go to the designer and be like:
'Make me a cover.'

I need to guide this person.

I have a certain idea of what the cover should look like in my mind.
I need the designer to make that idea a reality.

The first few times, it's very bumpy.
It looks awful and not how I'm picturing it.
But through the collaboration, we both begin to get a feel for each other.

After a few books in, I realized that explaining the cover concept with words was suboptimal.

Why not draw it?

So, I use Paint and create a very rough sketch of what I'm looking for.

This helps the designer out tremendously.

As I've been overseeing the entire book creation process, a lot of different things have been inspiring me.

One thing that's been inspiring me a lot are clothes.

I have this jacket that my mom bought me a while back.

It's lime green and dark blue.

I like the colors a lot.

I'm like, this need to be the theme for a book cover.

After overseeing the entire book creation process, I made a stunning realization.

'What?'

Viewing humans as books is a tremendous mental model.

I subtly broke down this idea in one of my YouTube videos a while back.

But the idea became more solidified as I've been working on the book covers.

Because the average person (in my opinion) has a very primitive view of the mind.

They think the mind is in the head.

Because that's where the brain is.

But I don't view it like that at all.

Let's use the language of a book.

I view the manuscript as the mind.
Is the manuscript only at the top half of the book?
No.
It's everywhere.

I view the cover, matte or glossy, as the physical body.
And I view the cover design, as the fashion sense.

What I found even more stunning is that we already use language as if humans are books:

'It's never too late to re-write your story.'
'Start a new chapter.'
'You're the hero that can tackle any conflict.'

Who is to say that the language can't be extended a bit more?

- The beginning of a new day is like flipping a page.
- Reprogramming the mind is like going from Read Only of a Word Doc to editing it.
- Empathizing with someone is to get a feel for the entire book rather than basing the book on a simple sentence.

Some may think this is an awful mental model.
These people would need to look at their own mental models.

There is no such thing as a *4* running around.
It's simply a concept.

If you ask a person where there is a 4, they won't be able to reference it.
They'll just gather other items and make a case for *4*.
All mental models are like that.

Stories to sensory data.

While with the book mentality, I can reference it.
I can pick up a book and break down my logic step by step.

Each book I write, each time I get more insights into psychology.

If I see humans as walking books...
I wonder who the author was.
That's a talk for another time.

BUFFET

A while back, I wrote a tweet on my Twitter.
Then there was a guy who sarcastically wrote:
'Wow, this guy has the answers to everything! Can you please teach me more about life?'

This was a loser's mindset on display.

I have noticed how narcissistic a loser is.
But often, they are depicted as wholesome in the media.

The people who are vilified in the mainstream are the winners.
People who show ambition, work ethic, and grit.

The narrative is:
Whoa, these guys got lucky.
Who did they screw over?
They must be snobby.

While time and time again...
When I run into a winner, I see someone who is a great listener, wise, and willing to share advice.

The loser has the 'me, me, me' paradigm.
This paradigm causes them to think that others create content strictly for them.
When they see content they disagree with, they need to be vocal.

"Personalize & whine."
^That's the battle cry of a tityboi.

I heard this spiritual teacher once say that being weak was a sin.
When you're weak, you make other people's lives difficult.

What makes good content?
I believe this is subjective in nature.

What someone finds good content is seen as ordinary by someone else and vice versa.

In my worldview, good content is content that is based on firsthand experience.
I don't just want to hear quotations from others.
I want to hear about *you*.

A while back, there was this guy named Victor Pride.
I discovered him late.
But found him nevertheless.

He had a simple writing style that I enjoyed.
He had emotion behind the words.

Then one day, I go to check his website...
And everything is gone.

I think he became very religious and repented.
This caused him to take down all his material.
I don't know how accurate this is.
It's something that I was told.

But I found that perspective strange.
If you are accepting a religion, great.

I believe it would be wise to share your firsthand experience with it.

What led you to it?
What tangible benefit has it added to your life?
How do you practice it?

I don't think it's smart to just delete your entire website.
But I don't know his personal life, so I won't comment more on the matter.

I believe in the future; more winners will take the responsibility to create content.
Because they do not have the 'me, me, me' mentality.
They have a balanced approach.

I know this one guy who hosts a dating podcast.
Cool dude.

He is like:
'I selectively choose a lot of outliers as guests. Because that's what sells.'

That's translation for:
'I get the fringes of people and portray them as the norm.'

That's how the masses get their world views.
They see something on the internet and are like:
'Well, if it's on the internet, then it must be true.'

But they lack media literacy.
Media literacy is to be ability to evaluate the **intent** of content.

Many people are not creating content to report back on firsthand experience and share truth.

Instead, they are:

- Hand picking the fringes and relaying them as the norm.

This is why I believe winners should create content.
Not to lecture others...

Rather, they are building something.
Learning something.
Spotting connections others are blind too because they are not chasing mainstream approval.

They are building a niche around themselves.

When an outsider discovers this person's content, the outsider will view the content from their own personal database.

The outsider will have a buffet style approach to the material:

- Take what works.
- And discard what doesn't.

IGNORANCE

When I was a kid, there were a few things I took as law.
One was:

- You don't step on the crack of a sidewalk.

If you did, then the other kids would be like:
'Ooooo, you stepped on a crack, now you broke yo' momma's back!

Younger me got scared.
I asked my brother if he heard the same from his classmates.
He nodded his head.
So, we decided to not step on the cracks of a sidewalk.

To this day, I subconsciously avoid the cracks.

Another thing I would hear a lot was:
'Now don't you feel crunchy?'

This was a translation for:
'You came off looking like a fool.'

Someone would say this if you tried to pull a fast one on them and failed.
Like trying to correct someone on something while they were right all along.

The last thing I heard was:
'You ignant!!'

Ignant was slang for 'ignorant.'

And people would say this if you were completely unaware of a
subject.

The first time I heard that was when I didn't know what Beyblade
was.

As an adult, being called ignorant is viewed as an insult.

Some would call it fighting words!

As of late, I learned that being ignorant can be a good thing.

And a lot of people in power often look for ignorant people.

Tom Monoghan was the founder of Dominoes.

He is one of those school of hard knock fellows.

Doesn't care too much for degrees.

If you can make a pizza with your bare hands, then he'll view you
in a positive light.

He wanted to make sure the people of power in Dominoes knew
how to make a pizza.

One day, Tom went against his usual hiring standards and picked
someone who never made a pizza.

Let's call him Jacob.

At first, Jacob felt out of place.

He didn't know how to contribute.

Sure, Jacob was successful in other fields.

But he didn't know much about pizzas.

One day, he was sent to a few Dominoes stores.

And each of the stores had these big machines that twisted
dough.

He didn't know what these machines were.

But he did know that they looked outdated.

That's when he went to Tom (the CEO) and was like:
'Hey, why do we use these outdated machines for?'

Tom looked at him in shock.
No one questioned him on those big machines.
Tom never questioned himself on those big machines....

The reason Tom never second guessed those machines was due to an emotional reason.

He initially went to start Dominoes with his brother.
But last minute, his brother chickened out and left Tom to handle the business on his own.

Tom was in for a ride.
Clocking in 18-hour days.
Failing.
Dealing with ridicule.
Rising once again.

Eventually, his hard work led to payments.
And one of the first items he bought with his hard-earned money was that big dough machine.

There was a narrative connected with that machine.
It was:
'Hard work pays off.'

Tom spoke so glowingly of those machines, that the other franchisees took the machines as the industry standard.
Dominoes was hypnotized!

It took a man who was ignorant on the field to wake them up from the spell.

When Tom was asked that question by Jacob, he had a realization:

'My goodness, I am so out of touch! Once I update the machines in all the stores, that will make Dominoes the #1 pizza store in the world!

And #1….they would soon become.

So, rather than being mopey about being ignant.

I mean ignorant.

See if you can use it as an opportunity to:

- Fuel more learning.
- Ask uncomfortable questions.
- And break people out of hypnosis!

That's how you turn a losing scenario into a winning scenario!

To be less ignorant, be sure to check out the Modern Day Polymath.

This book will teach you how to strategically navigate the internet, learn any topic you desire, and apply the information to your life!

GARGOYLE

There are 2 types of fake laughs in the social skills world.
One is the bad kind.
The other is the good kind.

The bad kind of fake laugh is when you are laughing nonstop.
This is typically caused from a state of emotional distress.

You perceive the other person to be in way higher position than you.
And you feel like a silence in the convo means you're doing something wrong.

So, you fill up the silence with sound.
You think if sound is there, that means likability is there.

Not always the case.

Instead, the other person is thinking:
'Why is this person laughing so much for? I didn't even tell a joke!'
That's the bad kind of fake laugh.

On the other hand, there is a good kind of fake laugh.
This is born out of being in a calm emotional state.

Don't you hate it when you are trying to tell a joke and the other person stares back at you like a gargoyle?
Mean face and dead eyes.

They probably had no clue you told the joke.
So, you attempt again.

And once again, no laugh.

The vibe is somewhat ruined.

I knew this one kid from my childhood who had the most contagious laugh.

He'd laugh in a way where everyone in the vicinity would begin laughing too.

We all know someone with a contagious laugh.

Not saying that it needs to be duplicated.

But think about what that laugh can do to an entire environment.

One thing I've learned over time is that sometimes faking a laugh shows supreme social intelligence.

It allows for the flow of the conversation to go by much smoother.

The other person feels comfortable around you.

This move should be exercised on the guy who is going for a rare joke.

Not the guy who is acting like a standup comedian the whole time.

If the internal world is calm when you do it...then this can be the considered as the good fake laugh.

Not the bad one.

Gargoyle no more.

GENIUS

A paradox is defined as:

-A seemingly absurd or self contradictory statement that when investigated may prove to be well founded or true.

A genius can perceive paradoxes, while a dummy cannot perceive it.

'Can you give me an example of a paradox?'

Sure.

Hardships will lead to an easier life.

This sounds ridiculous at first.

Hardships allow you to lead an easy life?

No way!

But let's investigate further....

1. Hardships battletest you & leads to thick skin (hopefully).

2. Thick skin = Creating an insulation from the world.

3. Thick skin = When internal world is stronger than external world.

4. A thicker skin leads to less stress.

5. What thin skin people lose sleep over, is harmless to someone with thick skin.

Now, the paradox of hardships leading to an easier life makes more sense.

Metaphorically and practically.

A genius appreciates it when life presents them with a paradox.

While a dummy is livid that they are not given a black & white answer.

In formal education, you are graded on black & white answers.

If you write *'it depends'* on one of your tests, then you'll fail.

However, in the real world, the more adept you are in a field...

The more you say *'it depends'* when someone asks you for advice.

The genius doesn't get overly cute with it though.

Sometimes, you can get so lost in paradoxes that you talk like a fortune cookie.

Always giving out riddles & making people think too much.

A paradox is like seasoning.

Sprinkle it rather than being engulfed in it.

I love the phrase 'Artistic Engineering.'

I never knew if it was a real phrase.

It was a phrase that rang in my mind one day, and I decided to write a blog on it.

If you type in 'Artistic Engineer' on Google, my article should be the first one that pops up.

Unless Google algorithms are playing with me.

As my article pops up, Google should presents a few people in history who were artists/engineers.

-Leonardo DaVinci
-Steve Jobs
-Buckminster Fuller

All individuals who were considered geniuses by their time & by history.

They had the artistic side.
The world of paradoxes, contradictious & huh???

They had the engineering side.
The world of logic, directness, & yes/no.

The combination is what them immortal.
The combination is what made them a genius.

IDEA A DAY

There are different definitions for an 'idea.'

Here is my definition

An idea is structured thoughts intended to make a point.

With this definition, I came to realize expressing an idea does not always require words.

I used to know this man named Leon.

He was a very bland man that didn't seem to have much personality.

If you got him talking about computers, that's when he'd show some charm. Other than that, a very stiff guy.

What my brother and I both noticed about Leon was this face he would do quite often.

It's when he would tighten his lips in a straight line, have his eyes dart, with a subtle head nod.

This move basically indicated, 'Well, this is awkward.'

He did this face so much that my brother and I decided to create an inside joke.

Anytime either one of us would do something awkward, we would do his strange face.

Just like that 'The Leon Face' was born.

After some time, this face started to be experimented on other people. If someone would say a silly joke around us, we'd tighten the lips, dart our eyes and give a subtle head nod, indicating...**well, this is awkward.**

Eventually the people who were having this face done to them were like, 'why are both of you guys making that ridiculous face for?'

That's when we would tell them about Leon...

After hearing the backstory about the face, they were laughing uncontrollably. They invited themselves into the inside joke. Now they started to do the face on their friends!

Just like that, the Leon Face became a hit.

It became wide spread within our community and friend circle.

But notice something....

The Leon Face does not require any words.

What makes it powerful is its lack of words.

This was an idea that was capable of spreading.

Learning how to communicate *without* words makes it much easier to communicate with words.

If you ask the average person whether they can get an idea a day, they look at you confused...

They are probably associating ideas to ONLY words.

They are looking too much at the formalities.

It's smarter to look beyond the formal formalities.

Do you think the first ever idea was expressed when words became popularized?

Doubt it.

Before words, ideas were communicated with the body. There are tons of variations that can be made.

If you find it difficult to express yourself, you may want to play around with strategies.

Rather than expressing yourself just with talking, see how well you can express yourself without talking. Can you create some sort of inside joke that is profound due to the lack of words?

Leon's face had a thousand words.

Yet, he didn't say anything.

If you can understand the power behind 'The Leon Face' then you may be someone who joins the Idea a Day club.

TIGHT PANTS

If you want to give targeted compliments, look at how someone dresses.

Some people dress up a lot. Not once in a while...Instead, it's the norm for them.

They dress up so much that it's taken for granted. Something seems off when you see them dress in a causal manner. *'Is everything okay??'* you wonder.

These people are very engaged in their fashion sense. It's almost like a chef who likes to cook a lot.

It's not rocket science that if you want to get closer to the chef, you should compliment their dish. Likewise, if you want to get closer to the person who dressed up, then....compliment their outfit.

They will like it because so many people nowadays view it as the norm.

Throughout my ages, fashion has changed a lot.
Around 2000s, it was all about baggy clothes for men.
Around 2005, big name brands dominated.
Around 2010, the tight clothes movement came.

The first time I saw a very well dressed friend of mine wearing tight pants, I roasted him.
Not only were the pants tight, but they were a bright neon yellow color.

How could someone wear such an ugly pair of pants in public?

Normally, this guy had so much style!

He fought back.

He said I didn't know what I was talking about. He said I didn't understand color schemes.

The neon yellow part, I could ignore.

What I couldn't ignore was how tight the pants were. It seemed like it was painted on him!

The roasting did not go on too far because he was very angry that I made fun of him. This is right before we were all about to go out.

I saw that he **identified** a lot with those pants. It was not just a fashion statement, it was an identity. This caused me to feel a bit bad afterwards.

I came to see that identifications happen very subtly for the person who is identifying.

For me, I really enjoy colored shirts that fit. Bright colored shirts with outlandish designs on them. Something about those shirts soothe my mind and make me feel more creative.

People make fun of those Hawaiian shirts. However, I love them.

Different people have different tastes.

So it wasn't right of me to make fun of that kids pants like that.

He taught me 4 lessons that day, but I am only going to discuss 1.
Identification happens in a very subtle manner.

This is a very sinister concept to be on the lookout for. This is
how wars are fought and groups are pinned against each other.
When one group begins to identify too much with something.

There was a philosopher/monk who said a while back that the
purpose of life was to fall in love with 1 idea and leave all other
ideas alone. Through that 1 idea, you'll find all the other
questions to life.

The mind may be like, *'Just one? Ha! I can do you one better and
fall in love with 4 ideas. Not a measly 1.'*

However, I believe this philosopher/monk was being strategic.
When you escape the 1 boundary, that's when you start to become
identified very subtly with other things...

It's one thing to like something...
It's another thing to let an object control the emotions.

1 idea is much harder than it looks.
When the mind has 0 idea what that 1 is, it's easy to fall for the
latest fashion trends.
Baggy or not baggy.
Tight pants or colored pants.
Maybe a bit of both.

A fragmented mind is a manipulated mind.

This friend was a mirror of myself. Just like he got mad at me for
making fun of his pants, I used to get mad at people making fun
of my colored shirts.
We were 1 in the same in different ways.

Remember the movie 8 mile?
Spoiler Alert.

Around the end, Eminem's character brings up all his flaws to the guy that he is battle rapping.

This confuses his competitor. Now the guy has 0 clue how to insult Eminem....

It's because Eminem already insulted himself which led him to liberate himself.

I told you that I was only going to share 1 lesson that I learned from my tight pants friend, but I'm going to share another lesson.

He taught me about the Jig Is Up Mentality.

This is the mentality of fear.

He was experimenting and took a lot of pride in his clothes. However, I think a part of him wasn't proud of his style.

Being somewhat competent in a field creates problems that you didn't have when you weren't competent at all.

Because when you weren't competent, you could not remotely distinguish right from wrong. Like the guy with the awful fashion sense who wears basketball shorts to a nightclub.

On the other hand, when you are competent, you're *aware* of mistakes. I believe Mr. Tight Pants was in that stage.

Pondering his mistakes more than his elevated fashion sense.

He had the Jig Is Up Mentality.

Otherwise, known as the fear of being exposed.

This fear is the feeling of being inadequate.

Competent people are susceptible to this more than others.

He gave me direct insight into what happens when you take yourself too seriously.

That was lesson 2.

Hell, let me give you one more lesson. Lesson 3 was on my end.

He didn't need to get so mad. I really was joking. Didn't want to put him down like that.

Lesson 3 is that many people who are clowning you are not doing it with the intention of ruining your self confidence.

More often than not, it's just for a source of entertainment.

We were all chilling in a small group, so I didn't think it was that bad.

When he got really mad like that, I was like *'damn, such a sensitive clown.'*

This leads me to lesson 4.

 I couldn't just stop at 3 you know....

4, is that intentions are hard to spot.

False Perception:

-Tight pants thought I was being malicious.

-I thought he was being sensitive.

Reality:

-Tight pants was suffering from the Jig is Up Mentality.

-I was trying to lighten up the mood.

These 4 lessons came from 1 moment.

Just imagine how many lessons can come from 1 big idea.

POWER

I want to tell you 2 stories.

At first, you may not see how the stories are connected.

But after some time, a few of you may see the connections.

My freshman year in college, I had a neighbor in my dorm named Ravi.

He lived right across from me.

So when I opened my dorm room, his door would face mine.

I didn't like Ravi's personality, at first.

He was in the ROTC program.

A very disciplined guy.

There was one day when the dorm supervisor wanted to have a floor meeting.

He wanted everyone in the floor to meet in one spot.

On the day of the meeting, all the guys met in one location.

The floor supervisor was nowhere to be found.

So a bunch of random guys who barely knew each other sat there in silence.

It was very awkward.

We were moving around showing our frustration wondering, *'where the hell is this floor supervisor guy? Who shows up late to their own meeting?'*

Ravi was late.

But he arrived nevertheless...

When he sat down, he noticed the awkward silence.

Within 6 seconds, he jokingly asked , *'Why isn't anyone saying anything?'*

This was a bold question to ask.

At least 35 strangers were there and he asked that question like these guys were his lifelong friends.

When no one answered him back, he was talking about how nasty the food on campus was.

The place the college students ate at was called *'Argos.'*

He labeled it *'Argross.'*

This got some chuckles.

Ravi's mere presence turned this very awkward moment into a chill atmosphere.

Soon, pockets of people began talking to a person across from them.

The silence turned into murmurs of chatter.

The floor supervisor soon came....

Story 2

This was a few years ago when I stared an athletics wardrobe business.

Had o fire for it. It was all about the money.

I had a brilliant idea for a logo.

I needed whoever I hired to make my thought, tangible.

Do not get remotely cute with it.

The initial guy I hired was perfect for the job.

He understood my job clearly and produced a mockup.

His mockup was great enough to be the final job.

No changes needed to be made.

Due to his competence, I decided that I wanted to work with him in the future.

As a few months went on by, I asked him to make another design for a product.

Asked him to use his creativity this time.

He typed back, *'What? So you aren't going to tell me what to make?'*

I said no, he could use his creativity.

I thought he was going to be jumping for joy.

However, he started to move scared.

It's like a part of him malfunctioned.

He couldn't fathom that I was having him do something where I didn't tell him EXACTLY what to do.

By malfunction, I really mean his mind stopped working.

The mockups he produced were atrocious.

It's like he did it on Paint, not Adobe or Photoshop.

I gave him a theme this time rather than strictly allowing him to use his own imagination.

Once again, that wasn't enough.

He didn't just need a theme.

He needed you to tell him EXACTLY what you needed.

I was puzzled.

It's like this guy can be Picasso one second, and the next second, he can't even make a stick figure.

He labeled himself as a 'graphics artist.'

But where was the artist??

Ravi and this graphic artist gave me a stunning insight into people.
'What was that insight?'
People don't really like power.

Watch how someone moves, not how they talk.

Due to plenty of rules and boundaries, there are limitations of power out there.
Otherwise, we would be living in the wild wild west.

If I just drove past a red light because I felt like it, then that would plant the seeds of destruction for other drivers.
Even if I drive past the red light with NO ONE else around.

When the floor supervisor was not present in the meeting, it should have given the opportunity for everyone to start yapping away.
But that wasn't the case.

If we all knew each other beforehand, that may have been the case.
However, when we noticed no one else was talking, we didn't even want our whispers to be heard among the strangers.

This graphics artist guy was highly skilled when he had rules given to him.
Yet, when the rules were taken away, it's like he was on the roads of life with people SEEMLESSLY driving past the red lights.
He was shook.

The world needs more Ravi's.

Just know, a Ravi can be seen as a tough personality to get along with.

You ever met someone like that?

Someone who seemed bossy...

Very blunt and to the point?

At first, coming across that personality may leave a bad taste in someone's mouth.

Especially, because this person is quick to call someone out.

However, when this stern personality leaves, their presence is the **most** felt.

It's because behind this stern personality, rested fairness.

Ah, the firm but fair individual...

Not all charismatic people are very warm and kind.

There are different types of them.

Some are like Ravi who thrive in power while others run away from it.

Remember, watch what people do, not what they say.

Last year, when the Corona virus was posting record high lockdowns, more people had time to be at home.

More power.

A few people capitalized on that moment by learning something new.

The rest were shook.

Like my graphics artist.

They were like, *'I don't have to go to the office? Then what am I supposed to do all day?'*

This same group also may whine when they are near the presence of a Ravi.

They may say something like, *'why doesn't Ravi ever let me make the plans?'*

Ha!

Because if you made the plans, then you'd self implode and give yourself a panic attack.

We all know a person like Ravi.

We all know a person like my graphic designer.

Power comes when someone takes accountability.

If Ravi asked 'why everyone was so quiet' to the group and everyone just rolled their eyes at him, HE would be the one living with that discomfort.

Others would have the luxury of laughing at him.

Worse, one of the silent guy's can now have conversation material with the other silent guy.

'Can you believe that Indian twerp was calling us so quiet? Like, what's his deal?'

The masses claim they want power.

However, their behavior proves otherwise.

If you want to be strangely charismatic, take away some power from others.

Not in an tyrannical way.

More in a gentle way like, *'fall back, I got this.'*

Their words may show discomfort.

But their moves will show otherwise....

CHOKE ARTIST

A few presidential debates ago, I recall a moment of a choke job happening live.

It was when Marco Rubio repeated the same sentence 3 times when Chris Christie pressed him.

I was watching that debate live.

As I saw it, I thought I was the only one who noticed what was going on.

I've seen this before. Where pressure can get the best of someone.
Either they say nothing.
Or they can't help but say something.

Rubio kept repeating himself, sounding like a broken boombox.

That's when the guy who was initially pressing him, **pounced**.

Chris Christie framed that moment as Marco Rubio being a typical politician who rehashes lines.

I thought I was the only one who noticed Marco's error...
But that was far from the truth.

Everyone that surrounded me was like,
'What the heck? Didn't he just say that?'

And the audience in the debate began booing him.
Undoing a lot of Rubio's efforts from before that debate.

Before that moment, Rubio was looking poised to be a threat.
In the first debate, I was living in Jersey.

And the mainstream media couldn't help but talk about him in a glowing fashion.

After that public choke job, Wonderboy had left the building.

This was a unique look into the choke job.

Something that is meant to cripple.

But can empower.

The guy who initially pressed Rubio, Chris Christie, was out of the debates a few weeks later.

Rubio, surprisingly made a small bounce back.

It seemed like he learned his lesson and was able to come back with humor on his side.

He gave Cruz and Trump some issues in one of the debates with his rapid wittiness.

However, the humor went a bit too far for some people's liking.

He eventually went personal in some live events and his humor was seen as crass.

This created a 'try hard' persona of Rubio.

Which showed that he will just do whatever is hot right now.

His core principles were questioned.

Still, seeing him bounce back from that choke job showed me that you can let dark moments fuel you.

I don't bring up battle rap too much on this email list. But in my opinion, it's one of the greatest resources for public speaking.

It's because you will routinely see a rapper choke in front of a live audience.

The audience boo's this rapper in vitriol.

You can FEEL the audience's rage and disappointment for having spent money for the let down.

And this rapper is standing their center stage in defeat.

The first time I saw a choke job was in the Loaded Lux vs Calicoe match.

Lux was seen as the clear favorite to win. He was a legend in the battle rap community.

However, he choked in his **first round.**

Not the second or third.

But the FIRST round.

That was just as shocking as seeing Rubio parrot away his line over and over again to Chris Christie.

The young up and comer, Calicoe, pounced on the choking legend.

Making fun of him and bullying him in the next round.

Everything looked over....

What happened in round 2 and 3 for Loaded Lux was nothing short of a miracle.

Not only did he bounce back.

But he went on to have one of the most iconic comebacks in battle rap history.

Chills down the spine kinda' moment.

What I noticed was that when I see someone choke first hand in a high pressure moment, it kind of makes me feel light.

'Makes you feel light? Are you saying you're happy to see them fail?!'

Not quiet.

The mind works through imagery.

It likes to **see** things.

A common fear before a speech is wondering, *'am I going to choke? What if I forget this entire speech?'*

That's when the mind may try looking in your data reserves for a moment of **you** choking to solve this question.

When you don't have a reserve, the mind may act like a drama queen and 10x a harmless scenario into a terrifying one.

What I noticed was that watching someone else choke was enough to soothe the mind.

It's lets the mind know:

 'look, Marco and Lux choked. But they didn't physically die. So chill.'

Simply with that level of soothing the mind, the heart becomes BOLD.

Very strange concept that I've noticed through watching the past presidential debates alongside battle rap.

-watch someone else choke and you feel less fear in choking.

I'm not one of those guys who says not to watch any form of entertainment at all.

I think using any form of information technology strategically can allow it to be a leverage.

Like watching a YouTube video or a clip of tough situations.

Seeing how that person dealt with it.

Then giving the mind the data points it seeks.

What's better is that with a baseline level of empathy, it becomes easier to make that other person's data point, *our data point.*

When I saw Rubio choking like that, I felt like I was the one on stage.

When I saw Lux choking like that, I felt like I was the one on stage.

Mirror neurons are the 10th wonder of the world.

Right behind Compounding Effect and the Pareto principle.

What we see, we can replicate.

The mind is a visual entity.

No need to feed it garbage.

But if you can find the lessons behind other people's mess, then it may help you out in the long run.

MY BIG TOE

One of the most influential books I have ever read was My Big Toe by Thomas Campbell.

Toe is an acronym for *Theory of Everything*.

Thomas Campbell is a NASA applied physicist and consciousness researcher.

A Theory of Everything is a theory that will unify the world of quantum with Newtonian with people with the mind etc.

Everything.

Thomas Campbell's book was impactful because he laid out a very simple theory and explained it very well.

He said consciousness was fundamental and that the purpose of consciousness was to evolve.

From these 2 simple proposition's, he derived time, light, matter, creation and much more.

The book is a 3 part series.

A trilogy.

'Okay...so? This is a communications newsletter. Why are you talking about metaphysics for?'

Because I'm sure the title got your curiosity.

I think Tom is smart because the book is very complex.

I don't recommend reading it if you think it's going to be an easy read.

It has math, physics, some technical jargon etc.

Still....look at the title.

My Big Toe.

Something about that is very appealing.

It sticks out.

If I didn't bring up that it was a book about the reality of life, would you have known?

Simply by calling it My Big Toe, Thomas Campbell grabs the attention of the every day man.

The group of people who aren't that curious about the nature of reality.

To take it a level further, the book is written in a way where he provides commentary to his **own** writing.

I thought this was strange.

I've seen people provide commentary to other people's writing, but to their own work?

That seems new.

Once again, he was being very deliberate.

This book has a ton of technical information that can make a newfound reader confused.

Especially someone who just bought it because they were curious about the title.

In the commentary sections, he tells stories and straight up jokes around.

EXAMPLE:

He'll spend 3 paragraphs breaking down complex systems, analyzing the speed of light, talking about the scientific basis for why we live in a virtual reality blah blah blah...

Then he'll bring in a commentary of, *'Hey there! I'm sorry, did I put you to sleep? Sorry, your crazy Uncle Tom has the tendency to drivel a little too long sometimes.'*

That sudden pattern interrupt from being technical to joking around brings the reader back & makes them more curious about reading on.

This is a NASA physicist who probably is surrounded by a bunch of logical people all day.

Talking facts, data and charts.

So him utilizing storytelling was fascinating to me.

To wrap it up, it's not a Theory of Everything without explaining philosophy, love and creativity as well.

This is something else he was capable of doing.

It took him over **30+ years** to write the book.

You would imagine that the more years added to take writing the book, the more complexity it should have, right?

Wrong.

The added years allowed him to understand what was important and what was junk.

I don't think he was a comical person in the beginning of the 30 years.

In interviews, he seems like a very serious guy.

He seems like the guy from the movie Matrix who created the Matrix.

Nowadays, he views life in a different way.

That's what writing a book & giving lectures on the book will do to you.

The point being is that you never want to think:

Oh...this topic is too complex, I can't simplify it.

You most certainly can.
You most certainly should.

During the process of simplification, play naturally creeps in.

No one calls their book My Big Toe and displays a big Toe in front of the universe without some form of play having been in the mix.

So make it easier on yourself.
Become familiarized with what you stand for and your ideas.
Get in the habit of expressing it to yourself and others.

Initially, it comes out very sloppy and not neat.
Remember, it took Tom **30+ years** to write his trilogy.
I'm sure you can spend 30 minutes for however many days.

Math is learned through being rigid.
Words are learned through being a child.

Use both & you may discover your personal Theory of Everything in the process.

GOOD KARMA

Karma often has a very dark association with. Pretty much implying that someone is about to get punished.

However, good karma is a thing.

Karma is viewed as an educative force that guides individual nodes (a person) to abide by the rules of a complex system.

-Play your role, and you stack up good points.

-Don't play your role (cheat, con others, put others down), then bad points come knocking at your door.

That's why I believe a good business strategy nowadays is to not be a scumbag.

Have some principles and stick by it.

I've had some good karma come my way.

It took me 3 years to notice it though...

This email isn't going to appeal to too many people. Yet, it may resonate with at least 1 person.

I want to tell you 3 stories and show you how they connected recently.

STORY 1:

The year is 2018 and a kid DMs me on Twitter telling me his girlfriend is toxic. He wants to know why he can't leave.

I gave him some tips, but he had more questions.

That's when I had an idea...

Told him to come back after 30 minutes.

In those 30 minutes, I released the thread known as '19 reasons why you don't leave your toxic relationship.'

He read the thread and could spot exactly why he stayed.

He thanked me, bought my Level Up Mentality book to support me and went about his way.

STORY 2:

The year is 2019.

My friend just quit his job to start a business to help teenagers with depression and confidence issues.

He asked if he can interview me for his new book.

His book was going to be the Tools of Titans for teenagers. Basically a complication of interviews from different people in different industries.

I agreed.

This friend was also my fraternity brother. So was happy to support him.

STORY 3:

The year is 2020.

A smaller account comes in my DMs and asks me if he could interview me.

I asked for what?

He said he wanted to interview me on the importance of having a personal website.

I agreed.

We did a quick little interview, he thanked me and I went about my day.

The year now is 2021.
Each of those 3 stories started off as seeds....
Now the seeds are starting to grow.

'What do you mean?'
Let me share what I mean by good karma.

MOMENT #1

3 weeks ago, I had 3 girls email me on the same day asking me similar questions.

Hey Armani, loved your post. Can I ask you for more tips on leaving my boyfriend?

Huh??

3 girls I never heard of ask me the same question.
Very strange.
So I asked them why they were asking me that.

They said because of my blog.
Which blog?
'The 19 reasons why you can't leave a toxic relationship one.'

I ended up turning that Twitter thread into a blog & posted it on my site.
I came to realize that Google was ranking me for the keyword, 'why I can't leave my toxic boyfriend.' Something like that.

Lol, that' wasn't my intention.
But hey, it is what it is.

A bunch of new people introduced to the ArmaniTalks brand in a very passive way. I didn't have to actively do anything to get that traffic. It just came from work I did a few years back.

That was a good look from Google.

MOMENT #2

Most of the people I work with are in there 40s. I got my first young adult client 2 weeks ago.

'From where?'

He heard about me on Amazon.

I was initially assuming it was from my book....

But no.

It was from the book on the teenage Tools of Titans.

Apparently, my fraternity brother who wrote the book is doing well on Amazon.

He is currently ranking on the first page of a popular Amazon niche for Teenage depression.

Guess whose interview is on the 1st chapter of the book?

'Who?'

Me.

MOMENT #3

I get a message on LinkedIn from this Bengali girl.

She wrote:

'Hey, I can't believe you're Bengali and from USF. I am new to USF and Bengali too. I just saw your site featured in a website! I'm thinking about started my site recently and stumbled onto your interview.'

She was referring to the interview I did on the importance of having a website.

The guy who interviewed me is now ranking for a popular Google keyword.

Once again, some benefits.

Good karma was calling my name.

It had been years...but it was here nevertheless.

I said that this email will appeal to probably 1 person because this person is probably in a crossroads.

The crossroads consists of the person wondering where their luck is? It's tough when the inputs don't match the outputs. Especially when you're working hard.

You put in the effort.

Help out.

Still, nothing to show for it.

I know because that was me a while back.

I was helping these people out, but I wasn't seeing anything back... What gives?

That's a law of the universe.

I wrote a tweet back which said that patience is a mindset, not just an act.

If you are patient with a shitty attitude, then you aren't being patient, you are simply waiting.

Good karma comes when you think it's never coming...

That's a lesson I learned from these 3 moments. Now mind you, the way I helped was also a big factor. With these 3 scenarios, I helped without immediately thinking, *what is in it for me?*

I don't always think like that though. Otherwise, people push you around.

I believe in taking if I'm going to be giving.

However, in these 3 situations, despite me not taking at the immediate moment, I found a way to get regardless.

In each of these scenarios, after helping these people, they were capable of helping me in the **long run.**

Good karma is a thing when we have a bigger picture view. The tough thing is that no one has the bigger picture view. We only notice it in hindsight.

If people immediately had the bigger picture view, then they would never commit a crime. If they saw the bad karma that was to come their way, then it would keep them on their toes.

Also, if they knew the good karma that would come their way, then they would mechanically do good acts, hoping for something.

The more I looked into good karma, the more I realized it wasn't about the act in itself.

It was about the intent.

'What constitutes as pure intention?'

When you are looking to help first and take second.

If you are looking to take first and are confused on whether or not you should help, that's when the intention becomes muddied.

3 moments.

Each moment took a while to notice.

That's how the supersets of the universe works.

It's a long picture view of things.

What doesn't make sense now makes perfect sense later.

Nowadays, one of the best business plans are the ones where you look like a crazy idiot for 5 years, and a mad genius on the 6th year.

This email was for the 1 person who was on the verge of quitting.

Now they are second guessing their quitting.

All the good karma seeds have been planted.

It'd be a damn shame if you threw in the towel before claiming your fruits....

BIRDIE

Yesterday, I went to get my annual haircut with my barber.
The appointment was scheduled at 10:45 am in the morning.

By the time I get to the shop, it's empty.
Just my barber on his chair surrounded by a bunch of vacant chairs.

I have a strange relationship with the Barber.

Normally when the shop is empty, we talk a lot.
I think he thinks it's his obligation to keep me entertained as I get my hair cut.

When the shop is full, we don't talk a lot.
He normally keeps to himself and I keep to myself.
Not only because it's loud with the clippers cutting my hair, but it's even louder with all the other voices having conversations.

Yesterday, despite it being empty, my barber wasn't saying much.
He was pretty quiet.

I liked this.
Getting my haircut is a chance for me to unwind. I consider it "me" time. I like it when he doesn't talk to me so I can just chill and unwind for 30 minutes.

When we do conversate though, it's nothing short of great.
We both have very similar personality types and interests.
So talking is fine too...

On this day, it was quiet from both our ends.

The TV was playing Vladimir Putin's recent interview with NBC.
I decided to listen to that.

As I was listening to the interview, I could hear a bird chirping..
Thought it was something I imagined at first....
Then I heard it chirp again.

I looked at the door & it was shut.
So no way can I hear such a clear chirping sound from the outside.

This led to me to 1 reasonable conclusion.
Is the bird chirping coming from the interview??

What kind of unprofessional reporter is this?
You are doing an interview and you couldn't even get the right location?
Tsk tsk.

I continued to hear more chirps & at this point, it was a foregone conclusion that it was coming from the TV.

Until my barber changed the channel...

The chirping continued.
Whatever this thing was felt very close to me..
The uncertainty made me more curious.

As more time went by, I finally looked at my barber and was like:
'Yo, you hear a bird? Or is it just me?'

That's when he turns the clippers off, smiles and says:
'It's not just you man. Let me introduce you to Roost.'

Then he pulls up a tiny, clear donut container and hands it to me.

Within it is a tiny bird chirping away.

That's when I asked him why he had a bird for.
He said that he found it lying around by his apartment, so he picked it up a few days ago.

Normally he keeps the bird in the house, but lately, he's been bringing it to the barber shop.
His daughter said the bird gets sad when he leaves.

Sad?
This bird can tell when you leave??

My barber starts nodding.
To demonstrate this, he leaves to the next room and the bird began chirping the loudest.

This animal was starting to build a bond towards a human.
Unique.

What I learned from that moment was 2 things:

1. You don't have a lack of conversation topics. It's more so the attitude.
2. Spot what is important to someone to make conversation feel like light work.

For the 1st point...
Yes, I could have created topics with him.
However, attitude wise, I wasn't there.

Just wanted to chill.

In terms of social interactions, if you find yourself having difficulty finding topics, don't immediately be like:

'Geez, I have nothing to say!'

You probably do have a lot to say.

The smarter thing would be to ask is:

'Do I currently have the attitude of someone who wants to be social?'

Sometimes the answer is no, and that's fine.

Being social all the time becomes a big headache and prevents you from enjoying silence.

Just focus on the attitude more than conversation topic materials.

If my attitude was feeling conversative, I would have immediately asked him whether there was a bird in the shop rather than waiting till the end of the haircut, pondering.

The next thing is to spot what topics interest people.

I could tell that not only did the bird build a bond with my barber, but my barber also built a bond with the bird.

Otherwise, he wouldn't have bought it to work with him.

When I asked him if I could take a picture of the bird, he enthusiastically nodded his head.

Implying that he was happy that I was showing interest in this animal.

This can be done in other facets of communication.

When you are running dry of things to say and your attitude doesn't even feel social, then let the other person do the heavy lifting.

This is a dynamite move though.

Don't make someone do the heavy lifting with a topic they have little desire to discuss.

For most people, that's discussing what they do for a living, where they go to school, and most formal questions.

On the other hand, letting someone do the heavy lofting with a topic that they care about makes **your** job easier.

Now it's just a game of asking some strategic questions, contributing every now and then, plus adding in a few well-timed jokes.

Birdie taught me that different people can get interested in different things.

I spent a little time after the haircut and noticed that Roost (the birdie's name) had some human like features.

Kind of seemed like a baby.

Maybe I was just seeing things because my barber hyped up the bird so much.

It's impossible to run out of things to say when you realize first hand that conversation materials are all around you.

LIAR, LIAR

Liar liar, plants for hire.

You ever watched SpongeBob SquarePants?
The cartoon.

That was one of my favorite cartoons when I was a kid.
It was of a sponge who lived underwater and had different adventures.

SpongeBob's best friend was a starfish named Patrick.
Patrick was a lazy idiot.
SpongeBob was this hyper dummy.
Their dynamic was hilarious.

Well, one day, SpongeBob and Patrick get into a fight. They are both accusing each other of lying.

That's when Patrick says to SpongeBob:
'Liar, liar, plants for hire.'
SpongeBob responds back with 'that's not how the saying goes.'
And Patrick says *'Well, you would know.'*

Patrick's statement implied that SpongeBob should know how this saying worked because he was in fact, a liar.

I want you to do 2 things right now.

1. Answer the question, what is your name?

Did you do it...

Seriously, do it and make yourself aware of how you delivered the response.

2. I want you to make up a lie about where you were this morning. Any sane person should be able to pick up that you are lying.

How did you deliver this?

Unless, you're a very skilled liar, you probably had some hesitancy in your voice for #2. Hesitance which was not present for #1.

It seems obvious why there is a difference in terms of delivery. It's because for #1, you were telling the truth and for #2, you were lying.

When we tell the truth (or are under the impression we are telling the truth) there is naturally a lot of certainty in the voice.

Want to know something scary?

A lot of people who are telling the truth sound like they are lying, while a lot of people who are lying sound like they are telling the truth.

I knew this guy named Allan. He was a very jittery guy with a great fashion sense.

For some reason, when a person knows how to dress from head to toe in a systematic fashion, they seem like a competent person to the eyes.

They seem like they should be telling the truth.

Allan's problem was that he had a soft voice and was an awful storyteller. By awful, I mean very awful. By very awful, I mean it sounded like he was flat out lying when he was actually telling the truth.

There was one time when he was supposed to drive me and a few other people to this volunteering event. However, he cancelled last minute. He said it was because his dog was sick.

The way he delivered the story seemed suspect.

'Hey man. My dog, it started early morning. Randomly starts pooping and not eating. It started early morning. My dog was feeling good before, but this morning, he starts pooping.'

Why is he keep talking about the morning for?

Why does the story seem fragmented?

Where is the continuous flow?

Why is there so much hesitancy in your voice?

Are you really telling the truth??

He was telling the truth.

Unfortunately, it took his dog dying for us to realize how serious the issue was.

The opposite is true as well.

I saw a very overweight woman on Instagram talking about how eating healthy is a narrative designed to fat shame people.

So much conviction in her voice.

She moved her chubby arms with the utmost ferocity.

Well timed words.

Brilliant eye contact with the host and the panel that she was speaking to.

Pure poise.

Only problem was that she was full of shit.

Doesn't take rocket science to see she lacked accountability for her weight and was looking for a person/entity to blame.

An impressionable mind would believe her.

An honest mind would ignore Allan.

This is a tricky situation for a communicator to be in.
What are you, some kind of mind reader?
How are you supposed to spot intentions?

Through body language and a holistic view of life.
Even then, a 100% success rate is never guaranteed.

After knowing Allan for some time, I came to realize the kind of guy he was. I came to realize his style of communication was very shaky.

I doubt I would have known his style of speaking at first glance. It required multiple touchpoints to get a feel for how he moved.

The multiple touch points allow you to get a feel for someone's body language. What is considered suspect for some may be considered normal for another person.

An example is the arms crossing the chest.
Some people use this move to close themselves off from the environment. Some use this move to show they are perfectly at peace in the environment.

You can do your own guesswork and lean a certain way. However, multiple touchpoints help spot the intention because you get a better feel.

Now with the chubby woman, I instantaneously was able to tell she was full of shit because there was a period where I was heavy as hell. Around 215+ pounds.

That lifestyle made me lethargic, sleepy, unmotivated etc. Not trying to judge her for being so heavy. However, there's a fine line on when to tune someone out.

Let's say there's someone knows little to nothing about fitness, has never been heavy themselves and is highly open minded. She see's the fat woman talking, and may believe her.

What happened?

Unfortunately, this person lacked experience.

This is why great communicator's have a wide range of experience and are well versed in multiple topics. Even topics that they don't really care much about.

Find the best communicator you know.

There are probably 1,000 unique facts about them that you would have NEVER been able to guess.

And that's still scratching the surface.

Do you pass the 1,000 unique facts test?

Or do people know pretty much all they need to know about you in the first couple of encounters?

If it's the latter, then chances are you lack experience.

Liar, liar is a tricky concept.

It's a strange world where truth tellers seem to be fibbing and liar's seem to be telling the truth.

It's just the nature of the game.

That's why the school of Hard Knocks has the word 'hard' in it.

Hard represents difficult.

If it was easy, then anyone can graduate from this school.

Difficult in itself determines who gets their degree and who has to come back for summer school.

THE TRUTH ABOUT TRUST

Socially intelligent people don't trust easily. They became socially intelligent in the first place by dealing with a lot of backstabbing.

This group knows the art of building rapport without revealing too much about themselves.

'Wait a minute bucko! I thought building rapport was all about revealing myself to the other.'

Nah. You're skipping steps homie.

And when you skip steps, you get snake bites. Let me give you a little social dynamics lesson.

You become socially intelligent by gaining social experience. No way around that. And when you gain social experience, you learn that the real world ain't all butterflies & rainbows.

You learn that there are a lot of snakes out there.

You learn that a lot of people do not have your best interest in mind.

Which is why you NEED a social filtration system.

The Social Filter:

-Stage 1: break ice

-Stage 2: break wall

-Stage 3: build rapport

-Stage 4: friend

Stage 1: Break Ice

This is the introduction stage. Socially intelligent people love to break the ice because it builds the social muscle & shows courage. A simple 'hello' is enough to get stage 1 started.

Stage 2: Break Wall

Now this person has no clue who you are, so they have their guard up. Your goal is to break thru the wall.

Typically, a sense of humor goes a LONG way in this stage. Keep the mood light here & avoid talking about real serious topics.

Stage 3: Build Rapport

See if you can find some similarities or get to know the other person more .

1. Humans love similarities. Signals to the subconscious mind that the other is not a threat.

2. When you try to get to know them, they warm up to you. Humans love talking about themselves.

At this point, you have an acquaintance! You should stop here for most people. Only a select few should make it to the next stage.

A small friend circle allows for more meaningful social bonds & less stress. Fuck the more friends, more popular mantra.

Stage 4: Friend

You have filtered out most of the people & the rare ones have made it to this coveted stage. This group should be:

-loyal

-helps you grow

-supports your mission

And there you have it!

- Stranger -> Friend

The more social experience you gain, the better off you will be in making intelligent social decisions. Avoid revealing too much to strangers like a tityboy & you'll have less snake bites on your back.

Filter correctly & you'll have the right circle in no time.

BODY LANGUAGE 101

Walk into interactions thinking everyone loves you. Your body language will automatically send off positive energy. Even if the person didn't originally like you, they may change their mind.

Much better option than thinking everyone hates you.

Understand that your ody communicates a lot of energy. Much more than your words. Let me explain the importance of body language & a few basic power moves.

Did our ancestors communicate with vocal language or body language?

'Hm.. no words back then, so body.'

Exactly. Human beings are visual creatures.

So subconsciously they see the body first & hear the words next. You are being judged by the energy you give off.

Want to know a secret? Most humans aren't paying attention to your words. You can barely keep pay attention to the thoughts in your mind. What makes you think that others are paying attention to all of your thoughts?

Truth is, they are not.

So it is your body that people are focusing on.

1. Humans are visual creatures.

2. Humans are emotional creatures.

If you want to be charismatic, you need to hammer these 2 concepts in your mind!! Luckily body language tackles both of these pain points. Now for some tips..

1. Smile

Smiling makes you feel good. Smiling makes others feel good. Mirror neurons homie. Just do not smile the whole interaction. You will look fake.

I typically like to introduce myself with a smile & sprinkle it here n' there in the convo. Find your sweet spot.

2. Palms

Palms wield power. Palms gives other people insight into your soul. So avoid tucking them in your pockets like a tityboy.

When someone sees your palms, they trust you more.

Note: AVOID POINTING. It's a gesture that threatens someone else's subconscious mind.

3. Eyes

Wide eyes make you look creepy. Darting eyes make you look unconfident.

Fix?

Strong contact with a light squint. Gives you a gentle touch. Breaking contact every now & then is fine. But break eye contact to the side, not down.

4. Tonality

It's not what you say, but how you say it.

Avoid monotone, soft voice, or aggressive tonality.

Work on finding your authentic voice. I highly recommend reading stuff out loud & recording yourself so you can become more in tune with your real voice.

5. Personal Space

Don't be that creepy person invading someone's personal bubble when you just met them.

You may not mean harm, but their primal self does not see it that way.

I can't give you an exact distance measurement to follow since it depends on context. Use your gut.

6. Posture

Poor posture makes you look like a bum. Slouched shoulders, dragging feet, heavy ass chin... all low energy moves.

Go to the gym & take care of your body. Your posture will fix in due time.

Also, try walking while balancing a hard textbook on your head.

7. Ticks & fidgeting....

Your body language communicates your internal world to the external world. Fidgeting is your intense emotions leaking out.

The best way to fix it is by becoming consciously aware when it is happening & fixing it on the spot.

Now I just want to leave you with 2 exercises to fix your body language if you have been struggling.

1. Talk in front of the mirror.

2. Record yourself talking.

Seeing yourself in 3rd person is a major key that will have you feeling super confident.

You'll see improvement in no time.

YOUR FUTURE SELF

No one will have your back as much as your future self. He or she is watching your every moves. They are speaking to you at this very moment.

You just need to open your imagination.

Put yourself in their perspective with your right brain.

'My future self is speaking to me?'

Yea. But you are unable to hear them because you're being too logical.

The reason your future self is your true mentor is that they genuinely want you to succeed while maintaining your authentic vision at the same time. The more you win, the more they win.

But speaking to that side is hard. If not impossible. For the logical person....

But the creative person?

Perfectly doable.

'How the hell am I supposed to speak to someone from the future?'

You create an alter ego. The alter ego is your perfect future image.

IMAGINE that person.

What do you see?

What are they wearing?

How do they behave?

Energy levels?

Keep going....

Once you have an idea, you will use your right brain (creative brain) to put your ego in their perspective.

'Well, that seems impossible!'

Which is why your creativity is powerful. It allows you to make eye contact with the impossible.

If I told you to imagine a flying Coca Cola bottle, you'd be able to imagine it.

How?

Nothing possible about that.

But like I said, your imagination allows you to warp reality.

Place your ego in their perspective. Now, look at your present-day self from a 3RD PERSPECTIVE. Got it?

'Yessir.'

Great. Now give yourself advice.

This will feel difficult at first. But it will feel like second nature the more you practice. You are EXERCISING your right brain.

Give advice to yourself in a concrete manner.

Write or speak the advice into existence. Don't just imagine it, yet. You need to work your imagination muscle before you just rely on imagining.

You aren't there yet because you are just starting this exercise.

Keep going.

Bend reality.

Make the future & present align.

CHECK OUT THE OTHER BOOKS IN THE SERIES

ARMANITALKS  

www.ingramcontent.com/pod-product-compliance
Lightning Source LLC
Chambersburg PA
CBHW050313160726
48002CB00001B/12